MODERN

TRAGICOMEDY

A Random House Study in
Language and Literature

CONSULTING EDITOR: *Haskell M. Block*

BROOKLYN COLLEGE OF THE
CITY UNIVERSITY OF NEW YORK

MODERN TRAGICOMEDY

*An Investigation into
the Nature of
the Genre*

BY

KARL S. GUTHKE

UNIVERSITY OF TORONTO

Random House · New York

PN
1907
G8

FIRST PRINTING

© Copyright, 1966, by Random House, Inc.

Library of Congress Catalog Card Number: 66–12534
Manufactured in the United States of America
By H. Wolff, New York

Für Dagmar

For I feel that, broadly and essentially, the achievement of modern art is that it has ceased to recognize the categories of tragic and comic or the dramatic classifications, tragedy and comedy, and views life as tragicomedy.

THOMAS MANN,
Preface to the German edition of
Joseph Conrad's *The Secret Agent*

Preface

This book is not intended as an outline of the history of modern tragicomedy. Although it provides some theoretical perspectives from which such a more ambitious work might be written, it is primarily intended to furnish a background for the study and enjoyment of tragicomic drama. It concentrates, therefore, on the theoretical problems that one should be aware of in any attempt to appreciate the genre.

Tragicomedy, defined in Chapter I as drama which is comic and tragic at the same time throughout the duration of its action, is a distinctly "modern," post-Enlightenment phenomenon. Since the reasons for this fact are to be found in certain aspects of the history of taste as well as in the development of attitudes of mind which were virtually unknown until modern times, the present study attempts to provide, though briefly, a glimpse of the aesthetic as well as the intellectual background of modern drama in Europe and elsewhere. While the bulk of modern drama is by no means to be labeled tragicomic, a significant and prominent part of it should be, and even much that is not tragicomedy at least approaches it in one way or another.

The term tragicomedy has for some time been bandied about with more casualness than responsibility. Mary

Lascelles, in her book *Shakespeare's Measure for Measure*, is, therefore, quite right in claiming that "tragicomedy has suffered in estimation from careless study and incomplete understanding" (London: Athlone Press, 1955, p. 157). The present study makes an effort to remedy the situation.

A systematic and comprehensive attempt to assess and analyze the theory and practice of tragicomedy of one national literature in all its ramifications and variations was made in my book *Geschichte und Poetik der deutschen Tragikomödie* (1961).

At this writing there exists in print neither a theory nor a history of modern tragicomedy as it is defined here. Yet there are four recent books that touch upon the subject in a tangential way. Marvin T. Herrick's *Tragicomedy: Its Origin and Development in Italy, France, and England* (University of Illinois Press, 1955) deals with the historical concepts of tragicomedy up to the end of the seventeenth century; but these traditional concepts, which are discussed in a section of Chapter I of the present book, are definitely a phenomenon of Renaissance and Baroque literary theory and literary history. They have no relationship to the modern concept of the genre, nor do they resemble it in any way. J. L. Styan's *The Dark Comedy: The Development of Modern Comic Tragedy* (Cambridge University Press, 1962) does deal with more recent mixed drama, but, in spite of its title, this book hardly goes beyond an appreciation of a few European tragicomedies and some isolated passages from various works that blend the comic and the tragic in one way or another. It is neither a theory nor a history of the genre. Likewise, *The Hyacinth Room: An Investigation into the Nature of Comedy, Tragedy, and Tragicomedy* by Cyrus Hoy (Alfred A. Knopf, 1964) is not a genre study but an attempt to show that one and the same principle underlies the tragic, the comic, and the tragicomic, this principle being defined as the contrast in the image of man between his ideal aspirations and the reality of his existence. Finally, Eric Bentley, in the chapter on tragicomedy in his book *The Life of the Drama* (Atheneum, 1964), revives historical concepts when he distinguishes two kinds of tragicomedy, "tragedy with a happy ending" and "comedy with an unhappy ending." These books led me to some useful material.

One reason for the scarcity of critical investigations of the tragicomic as a synthetic phenomenon (in which the tragic is comic and the comic is tragic) may be the fact that it does not appeal easily and immediately to the majority of readers and theatergoers. Or rather, it did not until recently. In this respect, it is not unlike the grotesque which was not dealt with extensively and definitively until a few years ago when Wolfgang Kayser published his book on *Das Groteske* (G. Stalling, 1957). The tragicomic is a difficult and, to some, irritating phenomenon to experience. As a result, critics were often tempted to discuss it, if at all, under the heading of "the aesthetics of ugliness," as Karl Rosenkranz did in 1853, or to discard it outright as decadent, monstrous, sensational, "manneristic," or as arising from a morbid nervous system. Also, rather a lot of systematic theorists of drama, for one reason or another, do not really catch sight of tragicomedy as a separate and distinct genre but rather speak of varying additive and unintegrated combinations of the comic and the tragic of the kind we know from Beckett's *All That Fall*, Anouilh's *Ornifle*, or O'Neill's *Anna Christie*. And then there are those who, in our own century and decade, repeat the notion of the more conservative eighteenth-century neoclassicists that the realization of the tragicomic is impossible *per definitionem*. And like their predecessors in the age of Enlightenment, they do not give any reasons for their

views either. Lionel Abel has reservations even about the
additive mixture of the tragic and the comic. He objects
to "this self-contradictory term," tragicomedy, "which
tells us only that humor and pathos may alternate in a
play, but does not define that kind of play in which
humor and pathos may alternate. Besides, if the events
on the stage are not irrevocable, then wherein lies their
tragic content? If the events are irrevocable, wherein
lies their comedy? The term tragicomedy implies, it
seems to me, two different kinds of plays, amalgamated
no one knows just how. If it is said: by the 'genius' of
the playwright—is that not asking the playwright's
genius to do the critic's task?" (*Metatheatre*, Hill and
Wang, 1963, pp. 32 f.).

But does this critic "do the critic's task" himself? Is
it not capricious to single out a relatively minor point,
the revocability or irrevocability of events, as the decisive criterion of what is comic and what is not—and
thereby tragic? First of all, can an event, as something
that has happened, or is shown on stage to have happened, be revocable at all? What Lionel Abel means in
his context is presumably that the event was or was not
inevitable. If so, one could argue the very opposite of
his theory: That an event which would theoretically
have been avoidable is, therefore, all the more tragic,
for example, Oedipus' murder of his father, as some ra-
tionalistic critics like Gottsched would think. And vice
versa, the appreciation of the comic may well be heightened by an awareness of the very inevitability of imminent comic disaster or conflict. Does not classical theory
of the comedy of manners insist on the unchangeability
of the comic character "type" (the miser, the vainglorious soldier, etc.) as a prerequisite for the comic
effect? If the "type" were not so predictably inflexible,
the comic effects would not be predictable; the predict-
ability, however, the anticipation of comic incident on

the part of the audience, is an essential aspect of comedy.

Whenever, on the other hand, the possibility and legitimacy of the tragicomic is admitted in dramatic theory, these discussions are usually in the nature of brief remarks, even *aperçus*, or merely amount to an expression of a writer's personal world view which is of little concern to the scholar interested in the aesthetic and dramatic problem as such. Also, critics easily fall into the habit of identifying the tragicomic with the humorous, the grotesque, the satiric, etc., or of identifying modern tragicomedy with the historical concepts of the genre or with the supposedly exemplary realizations of the tragicomic mode by Molière (*Le Misanthrope*), Hebbel (*A Tragedy in Sicily*), or by the eighteenth-century authors of sentimental comedy.

Unlike sentimental comedy, unlike satire and the historical tragicomedies of the Beaumont and Fletcher variety, modern tragicomedy, based on the synthetic phenomenon of the tragicomic, exerts high demands on the aesthetic sensibility not only of the audience but of the author as well. He must be gifted with a sense of the most subtle nuances and with an ability to realize them effectively in his work. Thus, there are not as many successful tragicomedies as one might wish there were. But we may console ourselves with the consideration that, for the same reason, effectively and perfectly realized tragicomedies are, invariably, the products of writers of excellence rather than second-raters. "Only the very greatest poet," Johannes Volkelt (1848-1930), the leading German aesthetician of his time, has remarked in his *System der Ästhetik* of 1910 (II, 560), "could succeed with the tragicomic in a fully satisfactory manner." The historian of modern tragicomedy will readily agree to this speculative assertion.

The present investigation, being a background study, cannot, of course, incorporate a large number of detailed interpretations of tragicomic plays, such as those to be found in the books by Styan and Hoy, and in various sections of Martin Esslin's *The Theatre of the Absurd* (Anchor Books, 1961), but it does furnish keys to the appreciation of these plays. It does not provide "condensed" interpretations of selected tragicomedies either, for these would fail to achieve their purpose since the success of any interpretation of a tragicomic play depends, of necessity, upon step-by-step, scene-by-scene, word-by-word elucidation of the tragicomic qualities. Such an endeavor, which I attempted in my book on German tragicomedy, requires more space than the present undertaking affords. The one interpretation that is incorporated into the text (Chapter III) as an exemplary demonstration of how to read tragicomedies is somewhere in the middle between detailed and condensed analysis, achieving, I hope, some of the virtues of the former at the price of the vices of the latter.

Every effort has been made to increase the readability of this book by keeping specific documentation to the minimum reconcilable with the responsibilities of scholarship. Thus, whenever possible, source references are made to the chapter or section of a work under study so that the reader may use whatever edition is available to him. It was hoped that references of this sort would aid the reader in his endeavor to verify or follow up a point.

Throughout the book, unacknowledged translations are my own; additions in square brackets are mine; italics are the author's unless otherwise indicated; and the orthography of quotations has been consistently modernized wherever necessary. The English version of the motto was slightly revised from *Past Masters and Other Papers*, translated by H. T. Lowe-Porter (Alfred A. Knopf, 1933, p. 240).

For the section in Chapter I dealing with the historical

concepts of tragicomedy, Professor Marvin T. Herrick's book has been useful. The reader interested in details of the development of tragicomedy as it was understood until the eighteenth century is urged to consult this work. Some of the source materials used in section four of Chapter I are taken from my essay in *Jahrbuch für Ästhetik* (Kölner, Universitäts-Verlag) listed in the bibliography, others from my book mentioned above.

My sincere thanks are due to my colleagues Bluma Goldstein and Philip M. Palmer for reading the typescript and suggesting stylistic emendations.

KARL S. GUTHKE

Belvedere, California
1965

Contents

MODERN

TRAGICOMEDY

CHAPTER

I

Towards a Definition

> *"Definition is indeed not the province of man."*
>
> SAMUEL JOHNSON,
> *The Rambler*, No. 125

The Elusive Genre

In the last paragraph of the *Symposium* Plato reports that at the end of the banquet, after nearly everybody had dozed off in drunken stupor, Socrates turned to a discussion of tragedy and comedy. "Aristodemus was only half awake, and he did not hear the beginning of the discourse; the chief thing which he remembered was Socrates compelling the other two to acknowledge that the genius of comedy was the same with that of tragedy, and that the true artist in tragedy was an artist in comedy also. To this they were constrained to assent, being drowsy, and not quite following the argument." [1]

One does not need to be a teetotaler to regret that the discussion of this fascinating topic ends on such a note of vagueness, for if it had been reported in greater detail, we would presumably know a good deal more, not only about tragedy and comedy, on which, of course, an irritating amount has been written, but also on the subject of tragicomedy, about which we really know very little. Clearly, Socrates must have pointed out certain principles, thematic, structural or other, that tragedy and comedy have in common. And if we had such principles, they would most likely be precisely those principles that form the constituent elements of tragicomedy. Knowing these, we might know more about the nature of a literary genre which has so far proved elusive, to say the least. And it has proved elusive, surprisingly enough, in spite of the fact that virtually all recent writers on the subject as well as most authors of tragicomedies since the eighteenth century are agreed that what distinguishes this genre is its "modernity" in that it is uniquely suited to an expression of the human condition as it is viewed in modern times.

To be sure, the word "tragicomedy" is not a modern one; it is, in fact, classical, and plays labeled "tragicomedy" have been published since the Renaissance. But, obviously, when modern writers and critics discuss tragicomedy, they do not have in mind the older meanings of the word nor the older concepts of the genre. Thus, while it may as yet be hard to state succinctly and comprehensively just what modern tragicomedy *is*, it is relatively easy, if less exciting, to state what it is *not*. One might do worse than point out these negative characteristics at the beginning of this investigation, for until the present day, in English-speaking countries especially, it is often the older concepts that we find when, in our quest for a definition of tragicomedy, we consult literary handbooks, dictionaries of poetic terms, and works on the theory of drama. The fact is, however, that these historical concepts no longer fit the plays that have in recent times been designated as tragicomedies in English-speaking countries and elsewhere, just as the adjective "tragicomic" has in recent times taken on a meaning which is anything but descriptive of or pertinent to "tragicomedy" in the older senses of the term. What, then, is modern tragicomedy not? Or, what are the historical concepts of the genre from which we should be careful to distinguish it?

Historical Concepts

The word "tragicomedy" was first used and, in fact, invented by Plautus—facetiously, to be sure—in the prologue to his *Amphitryon*. This prologue is spoken by Mercury who in his preliminary, descriptive outline of the drama calls the play a tragedy, then hesitates and continues, addressing himself to the audience: "What? Frowning because I said this was to be a tragedy? I am a god: I'll transform it. I'll convert this same play from tragedy to comedy, if you like, and never change a line. . . . I shall mix things up: let it be a tragi-comedy. Of course, it would never do for me to make it comedy out and out, with kings and gods on the boards. How about it, then? Well, in view of the fact that there is a slave part in it, I shall do just as I said and make it tragi-comedy." [2]

It seems clear from this passage what was Plautus', or at any rate Mercury's, reason for applying, though jokingly (as the Renaissance theorists and critics like Julius Caesar Scaliger already knew and modern scholarship has re-discovered) the label "tragicomedy" to *Amphitryon*. It was obviously the mingling of upper-class persons (if one may, at the risk of sacrilege, include gods in this category), traditionally deemed proper only for tragedy, with those lowly characters who had customarily been considered appropriate only for comedy. Clear as this Plautian meaning of tragicomedy is, it was ignored for centuries until the Humanist and Renaissance critics happily seized upon this convenient term in their search for some classical antecedent that might justify the apparent "irregularity" in their own dramas and in those of their contemporaries. These dramas, in spite of certain formal classical trappings, were in principle not

different from the mixed religious drama of the Middle
Ages which mingled kings and clowns and almost
everything else. Thus, their "irregularity" was precisely
that they did not conform to either classical tragedy or
classical comedy, but incorporated elements of both.
And, needless to add, the conscience of the Humanist,
Renaissance, and even the Baroque critic, troubled by
this fish-nor-fowl quality of indigenous drama (be it in
Neo-Latin or in the vernacular), was set at ease by the
classical precedent, no matter how spurious.

That this classical precedent was merely a word,
which had a specific meaning in its original context, was,
however, no cause for concern for these critics. They
unabashedly used it as a coat-of-arms lending respectability to all manner of mixtures of comedy and tragedy,
not only the Plautian jumbling of persons from all walks
of life.

Yet before we turn to a discussion of just what the
major forms of such mixtures were, it might be worthwhile to recall that it was not only the Plautian term
that, from the sixteenth century on, encouraged theorists and writers alike to acknowledge and even defend
the mixed productions that have always pleased the mass
audiences.

Classical dramatic theory as well as practice, of
course, drew distinctly defined lines between the two
basic genres, tragedy and comedy. Classical theory was,
in fact, fond of considering them in terms of neat and
accurate contrasts which would seem to leave no room
for an intermediate genre combining elements of the
two basic ones. As the *locus classicus*, in Cicero's *De optimo genere Oratorum* (*On the Best Kind of Orator*,
Section 1) [3] magisterially and quotably put it: "et in trag-
oedia comicum vitiosum est et in comoedia turpe tragicum" (In tragedy anything comic is a blemish and in
comedy anything tragic is ugly). The social class of the
dramatis personae was merely one of several distinctive
elements. Another was the level of style to be observed

and maintained throughout. Following the classifications
of ancient rhetoric, the lofty, dignified style was assigned
to tragedy; the lighter, commoner diction of everyday
conversation to comedy. Thirdly, there was the criterion of subject matter. As Martin Opitz put it in his
poetics, *Buch von der deutschen Poeterey* (*Book on
German Poetry*, 1624), tragedy dealt exclusively with
"royal decisions, manslaughter, despair, infanticides and
patricides, conflagrations, incest, wars and rebellions, lamenting, screaming, sighing and the like" whereas comedies were about "weddings, festivities, gambling, the
cheating and roguishness of servants, vainglorious mer-
cenaries, love affairs, the wantonness of youth, the ava-
rice of old age, pandering and such things as happen
daily among common people." Finally, there was the
criterion of the ending of the play: sad in tragedy and
happy in comedy; or as George Bernard Shaw stated in
1921 in his essay "Tolstoy: Tragedian or Comedian?":
"The popular definition of tragedy is heavy drama in
which everyone is killed in the last act, comedy being
light drama in which everyone is married in the last
act." [4]

These, then, were the principal markers of the sharp
dividing line which classical theory as well as practice
tried to draw between the dramatic genres, leaving logically no room for hybrids of any kind. Even so, theorists throughout the sixteenth and seventeenth centuries
could, with relief, point to various classical authorities
or antecedents which, if interpreted with more or less
reckless generosity, would justify the kinds of "mixed"
drama that, largely unencumbered by classical precept,
had developed on native grounds. Besides Plautus who
blazed the trail to a never-never-land where the extremes of society and even gods could meet, there was
Horace. In his *Ars Poetica* (ll. 89-98) he had admitted
that in the interest of decorum, that is, propriety of expression, comedy could on occasion be allowed to indulge in the tone ordinarily proper only to tragedy

while tragedy might at suitable moments lower its style of speech to that commonly reserved for comedy: "Nevertheless sometimes even comedy exalts her voice, and passionate Chremes rails in a tumid strain; and a tragic writer generally expresses grief in a prosaic style. Telephus and Peleus, when they are both in poverty and exile, throw aside their rants and gigantic expressions if they have a mind to move the heart of the spectator with their complaint." [5]

Inroads could be made even on the absolute validity of the seemingly less elastic criterion of subject matter. The classical antecedent here was the Greek satyr play, represented by the only extant example, the *Cyclops* of Euripides. Theory and model practice notwithstanding, this play did assemble amusing and sad, ludicrous and horrible persons, situations, and happenings in one and the same action. Horace, in his *Ars Poetica* (ll. 220 ff.), had in fact described the satyr play as such a hybrid straddling the dividing line between the dramatic genres, combining the subject matter of tragedy and comedy. He had not called it tragicomedy, but it was, nonetheless, a variety of what would later be called tragicomedy and was indeed called tragicomedy by Giambattista Guarini, the leading theorist of the genre in the sixteenth century.[6] As for the criterion of the outcome of the dramatic action, its claim for rigorous observance was weakened—or so it seemed to Renaissance and Baroque critics—by a passage in the *Poetics* of Aristotle. At the end of Chapter 13 he conceded that while he definitely favored the unhappy outcome for tragedy, there also was a popular type of tragedy which deviated from this pattern; and he did not expressly disapprove of it. This type of tragic drama featured a happy ending for the protagonists, punishing only the villains in the end. Euripides, though highly praised by Aristotle for having observed the unhappy ending in some of his tragedies, had written such plays which the later critics could use as grounds for the validity of the similarly constructed dramas of their own contemporaries, e.g., *Andromache, Rhesus, Iphigenia in Tauris, Iphigenia in Aulis, Alcestis, Electra, Helena,* and *Ion.* In refusing to denounce this kind of tragedy, Aristotle did, however, remark that its ending was actually proper to comedy rather than tragedy. He did not call this drama tragicomedy, it is true—he did not use the term at all—but writers and critics have done so from the sixteenth century to the present day, and the controversy as to whether this term was more appropriate than "tragedy" raged until at least the eighteenth century. It is curious to note, for example, that a man of letters like Giraldi Cinthio, who was the main exponent of this type of drama in the sixteenth century (a drama with noble figures, tragic emotions, gravity of style, a happy ending for the deserving, and no comic relief) ordinarily called his plays tragedies, *tragedias di lieto fin,* while admitting in the prologue to his *Altile* of 1543 that one might just as well designate them by the more current term tragicomedy.

These were the antecedents in classical theory as well as practice that not only encouraged the authors and critics of the sixteenth and seventeenth centuries to defend the "mongrel" dramatic productions of their time but also to apply the equally classical label "tragicomedy" as the ultimate sanction not only to the specific Plautian variety of mixed drama, but, to repeat, to all others also and to mixtures of these varieties as well. Some of the critics were consistent in this usage. But the fact remains that there was as much terminological confusion here as there was generally in the poetic theory of the time. Not only were semantically similar terms like "tragic comedy," "comic tragedy," "Mischspiel" (mixed play), and others widely used; to add to the confusion, "comedy" and possibly "tragedy" as well could still mean no more than "play." Even more disturbing is the fact that essentially similar plays could be called comedy, tragedy, or tragicomedy. Thus, to quote an observation of Marvin T. Herrick: "The *Theoandra-thanatos* (1508) of Quintianus Stoa and the *Christus Xi-lonicus* (1529) of Nicolaus Bartholomaeus were called tragedies; the *Christus Triumphans* (1551) of John Foxe and the *Triumphus Christi* of Schonaeus comedies; the *Christus Redivivus* (1543) of Nicholas Grimald and the *Magdalena Evangelica* (1546) of Petrus Philicinus 'tragic comedies.' " [7] Yet all dealt with the crucifixion and resurrection of Christ, a theme which, to be sure, allows for different emphasis, but otherwise not much latitude for individual interpretation or "novel" handling. Hans Sachs had no qualms about the subtitle of his *Kindheit Christi (The Childhood of Christ*, 1557) "comedy or tragedy"; and Nicholas Grimald, who subtitled his *Christus Redivivus* (1543) "comoedia tragica," referred to the play as "comedy or tragedy or both" in the dedicatory epistle. And to repeat, when the term tragicomedy (or one of the similar subtitles) is actually used to designate a hybrid play, one cannot and should not assume that it meant the same thing each time.

What, then, are the principal dramatic hybrids that are distinguished by the designation tragicomedy during the Renaissance and Baroque periods and, in some quarters, even in our present time? In accordance with the four criteria for separating tragedy and comedy discussed in the above paragraphs, there are four such hybrids.

First, plays which mingled *dramatis personae* from all stations of life. Second, plays mixing the styles proper to tragedy and to comedy as well as those which dealt with a tragic subject matter (*argumentum tragicum*) in the familiar language of comedy (*oratio comica*) and vice versa. Even Horace, who could otherwise be used so conveniently as a defender of mixed plays, had condemned this latter combination in his *Ars Poetica* (l. 89): "Versibus exponi tragicis res comica non vult" (A comic subject matter will not be handled in tragic verse)—and vice versa. The *Baptistes* (1603) by Cornelius Schonaeus is a play of this rare category. It is called a "sacred and new tragicomedy" for precisely this stylistic reason, as the prologue makes clear: "It can be called neither tragedy nor comedy, since it is a tragic argument written in comic diction. This is contrary to custom and seldom used before; for, as Horace declares, 'The banquet of Thyestes disdains to be told in verses that are familiar and proper to comedy.' Our poet, unconcerned about this admonition, has decided to exhibit a sacred history in a kind of language neither sublime nor ardent, but calm and sober, in speech truly fitted to the pious argument." [8] Third, the jumbling together of comic and serious incidents in one drama, the "mingling of kings and clowns" and matching of "hornpipes and funerals," to use the compact formulas from Sir Philip Sidney's unsympathetic *Apology for Poetry* (c.1583, printed 1595).[9] Fourth, a serious and potentially tragic play ending happily.

It is easy to see, however, that with the possible exception of the last type of "tragicomedy" (Cinthio's *tragedia di lieto fin*), these varieties will only rarely appear in a "pure" form. A play that admits the persons of comedy and tragedy alike would almost inevitably be constrained to mingle the stylistic levels as well; and it would, moreover, be susceptible to comic incidents or characters in a basically serious action. This mixing is especially true in the vast number of plays written in the sixteenth century in Western Europe which combined Christian, Biblical, and, more rarely, apocryphal subject matter with the formal, structural, and stylistic trappings of Terentian drama. Among the better known English examples are Nicholas Grimald's *Christus Redivivus* (1543) and George Gascoigne's *The Glass of Government* (1575). A good number of these plays, written in Latin or in the vernacular, were designated as "tragicomedies," "tragic comedies," "comic tragedies," "comitragic drama," "tragicomic drama," and the like. These terms do not necessarily mean that the plays were

in any way different from those not called tragicomedy.
But if they were dubbed with such a descriptive subtitle
it is often not easy to tell on precisely which grounds
they were declared as such hybrids; they would usually deserve these subtitles for more than one of the four
possible reasons. The happy ending or double issue was,
however, especially common in these sixteenth-century
Terentian plays written by Christian authors, as a survey of the principal subjects of the "Terentius Christianus" would clearly indicate: the fortunes of Joseph,
the prodigal son, Susanna and the elders, Judith and Ho-
lofernes, the prevented sacrifice of Isaac, the crucifixion
and resurrection. Less frequently, the sixteenth-century
writers used secular subject matter for "tragicomic"
plays, which are, however, aesthetically and formally
not unlike the religious ones.

As is frequently the case, dramatic theory sanctioned
what dramatists had put into practice. Some critics, it is
true, preferred to describe tragicomedy by just one criterion such as the happy ending or double issue of a potentially tragic play, or the addition of comic relief to a
serious action. But there were others who specifically
combined two or more of the criteria. This is particularly true of the Jesuit theorists. The Jesuit Pontanus
(Jacobus Spanmüller) in his *Poeticarum Institutionum
Libri Tres* (*Three Books of Poetic Principles*, 1594)
combined the Plautian criterion of *dramatis personae*
from various walks of life with the pseudo-Aristotelian
one of the happy outcome to describe tragicomedy.
His Italian colleague Alexander Donatus followed suit in
1631 in his *Ars Poetica;* he, by the way, gave preference
to the happy outcome for *all* persons over against the
double issue which punished the wicked and rewarded
the deserving.[10] The German Jesuit Jacob Masen added
the criterion of subject matter to these two criteria, al-
lowing the interruption of serious matter by comic incidents, thus arriving at a composite definition of tragicomedy in his *Palaestra Eloquentiae Ligatae* (*School of*

Bound Eloquence, 1654-1657). The decisive criterion, however, seems to have been the ending of the play, for in his passion for neat specification this Jesuit goes so far as to distinguish "tragicomedy" from "comitragedy" and in so doing he uses the outcome as the determining factor, everything else being the same. Tragicomedy, says Masen, "est actionis et vel illustris tantum vel illustris *ridiculaeque* permixtae conveniente metro imitatio ab infelicitate et commiseratione ad felicitatem et gaudium terminata" (Tragicomedy is an imitation, in appropriate verse, of an action, either merely exalted or exalted and ridiculous, which after unhappiness and lamenting ends in happiness and pleasure). Comitragedy (*comicotragoedia*), on the other hand, "est actionis vel tantum ridiculae vel illustris partim ridiculae per oppositum rebus metrum imitatio a felicitate et gaudio ad infelicitatem et dolorem aut ad utramque simul ab utraque opposita conversa" (Comitragedy is an imitation, in verse suited to the subject matter, of an action, either merely ridiculous or exalted and partly ridiculous, which turns from happiness and pleasure to unhappiness and grief or to both from both [opposites]).[11] The Romance languages seem never to have developed this concept of comitragedy, nor indeed the word, whereas in English the word "comitragedy" (according to the New English Dictionary: "a tragedy containing an element of comedy") did not occur until the second half of the nineteenth century and remained rare even then. Kierkegaard used the word in *Stages on Life's Way* (1845). In German, the word exists but is very rare.

Masen's clear-cut terminological distinction seems to have been observed by some Jesuit dramatists, and it was taken up by at least one secular theorist, Magnus Daniel Omeis, in his *Gründliche Anleitung zur teutschen accuraten Reim- und Dichtkunst (Basic Introduction to the Accurate Art of Rhyming and Writing Poetry in German)* of 1704 (pp. 228 f.). It was definitely new, even though the *term* comitragedy had been used

earlier in an indiscriminate fashion identifying its meaning with that of tragicomedy. Thus, among the few
plays of the "Terentius Christianus" ending unhappily
there was at least one "tragicomedy" (Schonaeus' *Baptistes*, 1603), and at least one "drama comicotragicum"
(S. Birck's *Judith*, c. 1540) ends happily, and Mathias
Holtzwart unabashedly had called his *Saul* (1571)
"Comitragedia or Tragicomedia as you like it" ("wie
man will"). Finally, Fernando de Rojas' famous dramatic "novel," the *Celestina*, was called, in the second
edition of 1502, "tragicomedia" because of its harmless
beginning and sad, tragic ending, that is: precisely for
the same reason that the Jesuit theorists of the seventeenth century would have called it "comitragedy."

To repeat: even with the Jesuit theorists, given to all-
inclusive definitions of tragicomedy as they were, the
decisive criterion seems to have been that of the ending
of the play. It is futile to speculate about the reasons,
but, as it happens, this pseudo-Aristotelian criterion
turns out to be the most important, though not the only
one, in the long run; by the seventeenth century it had
become increasingly dominant. In fact, the first time the
word "tragicomedy" was used after Plautus coined it in
Amphitryon, it was the subtitle of a serious play which
ended happily: Carlo and Marcellino Verardi's *Fernan-
dus Servatus* (1493), a historical play dealing with the
unsuccessful attempt on the life of King Ferdinand of
Spain. Plautus is mentioned in the preface as an authority, to be sure, but the reasoning in defense of the subtitle is entirely different from Mercury's: "quod person-
arum dignitas et Regiae majestatis impia illa violatio ad
Tragoediam, iucundus vero exitus rerum ad Comoediam
pertinere videantur" (because the dignity of the persons
and that impious violation of the royal majesty seem to
belong to tragedy, the favorable outcome, on the other
hand, to comedy). This example of the sovereign craft
of *ad hoc* interpretation then encouraged other writers
to justify their plays which ended happily by the same

devious maneuver. Luca Contile, in the preface to his *Pescara* (written in 1541, published in 1550), used Plautus in exactly the same unauthorized way, intimating, that is, that Plautus' criterion for calling his *Amphitryon* a "tragicomedy" was the happy ending of the play rather than the mingling of characters from the upper and the lower classes. So did Giraldi Cinthio in his *Discorso* on comedy and tragedy (1554). Cinthio wrote an impressive number of this kind of unremittantly serious plays which used secular, romantic themes and ended either happily or with a double issue. But he did not, except in the prologue to *Altile*, call them tragicomedies, preferring instead the Aristotelian label tragedy. So did his followers and disciples. But others throughout Western Europe during the sixteenth and seventeenth centuries did call roughly the same sort of play tragicomedy.

No matter how much these plays differed, the happy ending seems to have been a *sine qua non* and as such the most distinctive element. As Henry C. Lancaster has remarked in his history of *The French Tragi-Comedy: Its Origin and Development from 1551 to 1628*: "An examination of plays written in France during the latter half of the sixteenth century makes it clear, that the term *tragicomédie* could at that time be applied to almost any survival of the medieval stage which showed a happy *dénouement* and a form that was at least partially classic." [12] In the seventeenth century, by the time of Pierre Corneille's *Cid* (1636), the happy-ending requirement became *de rigueur* in France as the irregular form inherited from the popular medieval drama gave way to increasingly strict observance of the neoclassical formal features (though comic scenes were still incorporated even after the *Cid*). This development in French dramatic history from the "tragicomic" *drame libre*, using largely Biblical subject matter, to tragicomedy as the romanesque tragedy with a happy ending— from the predecessors of Robert Garnier and Alexandre Hardy to Corneille—has been traced by Marvin T.

Herrick in his book on pre-eighteenth-century tragi-comedy in Italy, France, and England.

Much the same could be said of English (as well as German) tragicomedy in the sixteenth and seventeenth centuries. As Sir Philip Sidney put it in his *Apology for Poetry*, English plays of the time were "neither right tragedies nor right comedies," mingling, as they did, kings and clowns and thus turning out to be "mongrel tragicomedy." [13] It is true that this hybrid irregular drama growing out of the native plays of the Middle Ages was widely termed "tragicomedy." It is also unde-niable that in England the neoclassical rules, one of which described tragicomedy as tragedy with a happy ending, were never accepted as fully as they had been in France.[14] But even so, just as in France and Germany, the happy *dénouement* came to be the most conspicuous trademark of the genre in England as well. The best known English exponents of full-fledged tragicomedy are, of course, Francis Beaumont and John Fletcher who perfected tragicomedy as it was known at the time and made it a popular as well as respectable form of enter-tainment.[15]

Thus, French, German, and, to a lesser extent, English tragicomedy, arising by the early or mid-seventeenth century from the indiscriminately jumbled *drame libre* of the native tradition, had, in its development towards increasingly stricter adherence to the neoclassic rules, come close to what tragicomedy had meant in Italy all along: namely, neoclassical tragedy with a happy end-ing, as Cinthio had written it in the previous century. (The other variety of Italian tragicomedy was the pas-toral play created by Guarini which will be discussed below.) The only difference was that Cinthio and his school had consistently refused to admit comic materials of any kind. These comic elements of the native tradi-tion dwindled to the vanishing point in French and Ger-man tragicomedy, but they were never eliminated en-tirely.

To sum up, let us ask what is the overall impression that we have of seventeenth-century European tragicomedy at the peak of its development. In several respects it is very much like romantic comedy and melodrama. More often than not, it turns on a romantic love intrigue which leads us into faraway outlandish settings and taxes our sense of probability with the most unlikely happenings and situations and far-fetched juxtapositions of the ludicrous and the serious. The plot is usually intricate and contrived, invariably reaching its triumph of artistry in the *dénouement*. In fact, its most characteristic and conspicuous feature is the skillful manipulation of the happy outcome. Dramatists exert an ingenuity as stupendous as that of Hollywood scriptwriters in order to maintain suspense until the very last moment, only to break it by the most unexpected reversals of fortune, suggesting a not so graceful tribute to the charitable cause of poetic justice. Poison will turn out to have been a harmless sleeping potion; the identities will be revealed of infants kidnapped by pirates and raised in obscurity by shepherds or of infants exchanged at birth; tyrants will die a timely death; and even more moving, despots will be overcome by sudden repentance, generosity, and resignation. Even ghosts *ex machina* are not unheard of, or villainy is discovered at the last moment and the villain banished to remote lands. The dead will wake up in the nick of time; disguises are revealed; a crucial *dramatis persona* may even fall to his death through a trapdoor at a critical moment, as in Thomas Middleton's *Witch;* and so on.

Once this type of tragicomedy—most ably represented by Beaumont and Fletcher in England, Adolf von Haugwitz and Johann Christian Hallmann in Germany, Garnier, Hardy, Jean de Mairet and Jean de Rotrou in France—is established, it is hard to see how an audience, trained to know what to expect, can take seriously everything potentially tragic that precedes the conclusion of the play. The audience knows that all complications will be resolved in the end, and it is, therefore, primarily interested in the precise manner in which the avoidance of imminent disaster is contrived. In other words, the audience tends to develop the mentality of the reader of the cheaper detective stories of a later day. One cannot but wonder if this appeal is one of the reasons for the immense popularity of this kind of entertainment in the seventeenth century and the consequent decline of the vogue in the eighteenth century. At any rate, since the eighteenth century what has been termed "tragicomedy" bears no resemblance whatsoever to what tragicomedy was when it had its heyday in Western Europe.

Before we turn to modern tragicomedy and its problems, we should have a brief glimpse of one more variety of tragicomedy produced in the sixteenth century: Guarini's pastoral tragicomedy, which was widely imitated on the continent and in England (Alexandre Hardy, Jean de Mairet, Ben Jonson, Samuel Daniel, John Fletcher, E. C. Homburg). This was not just "tragicomedy" (as the term was understood at the time) in the guise of pastoral setting and pastoral *personae*. To be sure, it, too, was a conglomeration of elements traditionally reserved for tragedy and comedy. But what the Italian Renaissance critic aims at in his treatises in defense of his own controversial pastoral tragicomedy, *Il Pastor Fido* (1590), is a less "hybrid" dramatic genre. Whereas the other types of tragicomedy discussed above incorporated some of the *extremes* of tragedy and comedy, that is, elements exclusively peculiar to comedy or to tragedy, Guarini's concept of tragicomedy provided only for the adoption and harmonizing of the less extreme and, therefore, more easily compatible elements of the two dramatic genres. It, thus, anticipated, in principle, the procedure of the eighteenth-century writers of sentimental comedy, *comédie larmoyante*, *weinerliches Lustspiel*, the more so because Guarini correctly considered the pastoral trappings as inessential to his concept of tragicomedy. Much like later critics such as Richard Steele, Denis Diderot, Sébastien Mercier, Joseph Trapp, and Christian Fürchtegott Gellert, Guarini combined in his concept of tragicomedy the mildly tragic and the mildly comic emotions, the mildly tragic and the mildly comic motifs, the mildly "tragic" and the mildly "comic" levels of style. The *dramatis personae*—shepherds and shepherdesses, satyrs and nymphs, and descendants of gods settled in an Arcadia remote from anybody's "reality"—were not the characters familiar in tragedy or comedy. The outcome was to be a single, happy one in all events. As Guarini writes: "He who composes tragicomedy takes from tragedy its great persons but not its action, its verisimilar plot but not its true one, its movement of the feelings but not its disturbance of them, its pleasure but not its sadness, its danger but not its death; from comedy laughter that is not excessive, modest amusement, feigned difficulty, happy reversal, and above all the comic order." [16]

Sentimental Comedy

If, as pointed out above, the eighteenth century began to develop what we have called "modern" tragicomedy, it also produced the sentimental drama which is essentially close to the Guarini type of tragicomedy. We could ignore this aspect of dramatic history of the Enlightenment if it were not for the fact that this type of drama was frequently called tragicomedy in the eighteenth century and is still regarded as such by some contemporary critics. Thus, Allardyce Nicoll, in his influential *Theory of Drama*, discusses sentimental comedy in a chapter entitled "Tragi-comedy." So does, among others, Marvin T. Herrick in his chapter on the "Aftermath of Tragicomedy." Historically speaking, this classification is not incorrect as it follows what was contemporary usage, though it was by no means unanimous. Johann Christoph Gottsched, the leading German theo-

rist in Enlightenment poetics, designated "cet équi-
voque enfant" (as Nivelle de la Chaussée called sentimental comedy in his *Critique de la Fausse Antipathie*,
1734) as tragicomedy in his *Critische Dichtkunst*
(fourth edition, 1751, p. 650). Johann Heinrich Zedler
had done the same in the monumental *Universallexikon*
of 1745; so had Pierre-Matthieu-Martin de Chassiron in
his *Réflexions sur le comique-larmoyant* of 1749, to mention just a few.

Noting the historical label is one thing, but retaining
it is quite another. If we let ourselves be guided for the
time being by the word tragicomedy, which clearly implies a mingling of elements of both basic dramatic
genres, it would indeed be arbitrary to identify with
this label a drama which occupies the middle ground *between* tragedy and comedy and rarely, if ever, touches
the extremes of comedy or tragedy. At any rate, this is
how sentimental comedy, minor variations within the
genre notwithstanding, was defined in England, France,
and Germany throughout the eighteenth century. The
leading theorists of sentimental comedy, such as the
Englishman Joseph Trapp (*Praelectiones Poeticae*,
1722), Bernard de Fontenelle (*Préface générale* to Volume 7 of his *Oeuvres*, 1751), Gellert (*Pro Comoedia
commovente Commentatio*, 1751), Denis Diderot (*En-
tretiens sur le Fils Naturel*, 1757; *De la poésie dramatique*, 1758), Pierre Augustin Carron de Beaumarchais
(*Essai sur le genre dramatique sérieux*, 1767), and Louis
Sébastien Mercier (*Du théâtre, ou nouvel essai sur l'art
dramatique*, 1773), are all careful to insist that the new
genre is not a combination of comedy and tragedy (and,
therefore, as Diderot insists, *not* tragicomedy), in fact,
neither tragedy nor comedy, but a third, intermediate
type, which neither Thalia nor Melpomene could claim
to be theirs—as Chaussée put it in his *Critique de la
Fausse Antipathie*.

And rightly so, for instead of tragic pity and fear, sentimental drama arouses a considerably toned-down vari-

ety of sympathy for the indefatigably virtuous and often priggishly Grandisonian protagonists; it arouses a "joy too exquisite for laughter" (Richard Steele's preface to his *Conscious Lovers*, 1723) over their typical contests in vociferous magnanimity. And when sentimental comedy, unlike Chaussée's, allowed an admixture of something "funny," it was hardly anything mordantly ludicrous as in the comedy of manners of the time, but rather motifs which caused, instead of laughter, a tempered, mild, and tender kind of half-smile. Zedler was right when he missed anything "comedy-like" in the *comédie larmoyante*. Sentimental comedy in all its variations throughout Europe was, in the last analysis, essentially a tearfully edifying glorification of the eighteenth-century bourgeois concept of virtue and respectability, often burdened by improbability of plot and character alike, and hardly enlivened by its specific moral teachings. Occupying the neutral middle ground *between* tragedy and comedy rather than comprising the territory of comedy *and* tragedy, the sentimental "comedy" of the age of Enlightenment was in fact virtually *drame*. This is indeed what it was called at the time by some critics, e.g., Beaumarchais and Mercier, who rejected the term *tragicomédie* as unsuitable.[17] Unsuitable it is; and this is not quibbling, for if one chooses, as Herrick and others have done, to expand the meaning of "tragicomedy" to include not only the various historical concepts of the genre that we have sketched, but also any and all kinds of intermediate dramatic genres, one lumps together too many different types of plays and creates a confusion in which very little, if anything, is gained. We would need to accept statements like Herrick's: Ibsen's *A Doll's House* "is hardly a tragedy. It cannot be called pure comedy. . . . The *Doll's House* is tragicomic; it lies between tragedy and comedy; it is a *drame*" (p. 320). This explanation would presuppose that tragicomedy has, paradoxically, nothing to do with either tragedy or comedy. That, however, is not only at odds with what the word, at face value, implies, but, more importantly, also with current usage of the words tragicomic and tragicomedy as well as with the plays that have, in recent times, been so labeled. This is not only a matter of terminology. It affects, moreover, our entire concept of the development of modern drama, for while it may be true that "most of the significant modern dramas still occupy a middle ground between tragedy and comedy," it does not follow that "the spirit of tragicomedy continued to live [since the seventeenth century] and still lives," as Herrick states in his conclusion (pp. 320 f.). It would be useful to make more careful distinctions. For example, if we agree that Ibsen's *A Doll's House* is "between" tragedy and comedy, we do not need to assume that Chekhov's *The Cherry Orchard* is "between" the genres in the same manner, as Professor Herrick would have us think (p. 320). Even if it really is the kind of intermediate *drame* which would put it uncomfortably close to sentimental comedy, *A Doll's House* would hardly deserve the designation tragicomedy; *The Cherry Orchard* would, as it embraces both extreme comedy and extreme tragedy, in addition to covering the middle ground. While the most significant modern dramas may occupy the middle ground between tragedy and comedy, they are by no means all written in the vein of *The Cherry Orchard*. Or else the history of modern drama would be the history of tragicomedy, which it is not. It certainly includes it, but it is not identical with it.

A Question of Taste: The Critical Attitudes of Neoclassicism

The discussion of sentimental comedy has given us one clue to the nature of "modern" tragicomedy: true to its name, it presents a mixture of the effects of comedy and tragedy. Unlike the *comédie larmoyante*, it embodies the tragic as well as the comic, in a manner which we shall leave unspecified for the time being. Now, the types of "tragicomedy" discussed as "Historical Concepts" do, as a rule, incorporate "tragic" as well as "comic" scenes, persons, and events. Yet these plays are by and large a phenomenon of the sixteenth and seventeenth centuries. By 1700 they have all but disappeared whereas "modern" tragicomedy is essentially a matter of the nineteenth and twentieth centuries. More than that: while both periods offer dramas combining elements of tragedy and comedy which are basically unlike the intermediate genre, that is, the sentimental comedy, the nature of the combination is crucially different. Before, however, the new mode of mingling the comic and the tragic could be brought about in the nineteenth century, a protracted and lively debate took place among critics about the justifiability of *any* kind of mixture of the elements of comedy and tragedy. In fact, the "mongrel" drama was one of the major bones of contention in the critical in-fighting of the neoclassical age throughout Western Europe. It is entirely erroneous to assume, as it is in the prestigious *Reallexikon der deutschen Literaturgeschichte*, that neoclassicist theory rigorously rejected "tragicomedy," treating it as a "bastard genre which was to be excluded from any serious discussion" (IV, 97). On the contrary, the critical investigations of neoclassicist critics paved the way not only for the aesthetic appreciation of the, by now, time-honored additive mingling of extreme elements of tragedy and comedy but, more significantly, also for that synthetic union of these two elements which creates a virtual identity of both, where the comic is the tragic and the tragic the comic. This, however, is a "modern" phenomenon in the sense that we have used that term so far. Thus, neoclassicism, in its appreciation of such hybrid forms that had otherwise been considered "gothic," barbaric, and distasteful, made a very significant contribution to the rise of a distinctly modern form of literature. It would, therefore, seem desirable to sketch the manner in which this case for tragicomedy is made in the late seventeenth and throughout the eighteenth century.

To begin with, this period of European literary criticism was singularly well qualified to initiate a positive critical appreciation of the mixture of comedy and tragedy. It was then that the "rules" of traditional criticism, first formulated as such by Italian Renaissance critics and interpreters of classical authorities as Lodovico Castelvetro and ordinarily referred to as stringently binding norms of literary creation, were at last put to the test. They were put to the test of "reason," that is, of the generously interpreted principle of "imitation of nature" and the psychological and aesthetic "laws" of our reception of or reaction to literature. The "rules" had in effect banned any mixture of the comic and the tragic whatsoever. Reason, however, did not necessarily follow suit, for whereas earlier criticism, which discussed tragicomedy (whether defending or rejecting it), had consistently operated with easily distinguishable and definable structural elements of the two basic genres—the social class of the *dramatis personae*, the funny and the sad scenes, the happy and the unhappy outcome of the action—neoclassical criticism, in its more liberal and, hence, historically more significant quarters, begins to concentrate instead on the nature and peculiarities of the "aesthetic sense" of man and its inclination or disinclination to appreciate the mixture of the comic and the tragic as aesthetically pleasing. And to the "aesthetic sense," neoclassicist criticism finds, this mixture is indeed pleasing; the old concept of imitation of nature as a principle of literature is, in fact, reinterpreted in accordance with this preference.

To be sure, this change in outlook and orientation did not automatically result in applause for such a mixture. On the contrary, it was equally possible for an eighteenth-century critic to arrive at the opposite conclusion, namely, that the traditional "rules" were based on reason and "certainly derived from the depth of the nature of man," as Christian Felix Weisse put it apodictically in 1776 in the preface to his *Trauerspiele*. Even the example of Shakespeare would, in Weisse's case, not allow a modification of this view, and rigorously neoclassicist critics like Réné Rapin (*Réflexions sur l'éloquence et la poétique*, 1674) and Thomas Rymer (*The Tragedies of the Last Age*, 1678; *A Short View of Tragedy*, 1693) would have agreed wholeheartedly. "Discordant emotions are unpleasant when jumbled together," Henry Home (Lord Kames) states flatly in his *Elements of Criticism* (1762).[18] Given such estimates of the juxtaposition (rather than fusion) of elements of tragedy and comedy, it is hardly surprising that the even more subtle mixture, the *identity* of tragic fear and comic laughter, that is, the quality that distinguishes modern tragicomedy, could meet with even less appreciation in some neoclassicist circles. In his *Réflexions sur le comique-larmoyant* (1749) Chassiron asserts with an air of self-evident authority: "To either laugh or cry according to the different feelings of the heart are no doubt natural sensations; but laughing and crying at one and the same moment . . . is not at all according to nature." [19] (Some of Molière's comedies, especially *Le Misanthrope*, *Tartuffe*, and possibly *Georges Dandin*, would, one would think, have given Chassiron some second thoughts on the matter. But this reminder is historically unfair, for one should remember that the undercurrent of tragedy which modern critics tend to see in these comedies was almost generally overlooked at the time. Or is it there at all? And if so, in spite of Molière's intentions or because of them?)

The same negative stand on the problem of the mixture of the elements of comedy and tragedy was possible and, indeed, widespread in the eighteenth century when it was approached from the vantage point of the principle of "imitation of nature." What precisely this "nature" is that is to be imitated by the poet is a matter for the theorist to decide beforehand, and, more often than not, critics of the neoclassical period narrowed the idea of nature in such contexts to "beautiful" nature. Beautiful nature, however, was nature organized in a rational manner, *not* the jumble of contrasts and incongruities that make up our everyday life. The latter, on the contrary, was definitely considered "ugly," and the mingling of the tragic and the comic was merely one such instance of the ugly, which, in the view of the more conservative neoclassical critics, was to be kept out of literature at all cost. In other words, by and large, beautiful nature, as the object of poetic imitation, was a conscious stylization of reality which banished tragicomedy —no matter how defined—from the realm of acceptable literature.

We wonder what principle lay behind such an *a priori* condemnation of the union of the elements and effects of the two basic dramatic genres. The answer is to be found in that ubiquitous word "taste" (*gusto, goût, Geschmack*) which is bandied about so much in neoclassical criticism. It is in the background of all the discussions on poetics in this period. This is not surprising, for the concept of "taste" is related, on the one hand, to the seemingly more objective principle of imitation of nature and, on the other hand, again by way of reason, to the entire complex of hard-to-define psychoaesthetical "laws" governing the individual in his appreciation of literature. The first link is clearly established, for example, by Charles Batteux in the beginning of his *Les beaux arts réduits à un même principe* (*The Fine Arts Reduced to a Single Principle,* 1746) when he says, "that taste, for which the arts are made and which is their judge, should be satisfied when nature is well chosen and well imitated by the arts" (p. 9). The other link, as Alfred Bäumler's[20] detailed discussion shows, can be seen in the universally held notion that the intuitive, emotional judgment of taste is, in the last analysis, merely an instantaneous and unreflected anticipation of the judgment of reason. Thus, taste was essentially an *analogon rationis*.

Taste decides what is beautiful and what is not. And it is from the neoclassicist debate about taste that one can understand most clearly why it is that tragicomedy is not considered a "beautiful" literary genre. Again and again the concept of "harmony" turns up in these discussions of literary *goût*. Harmony is, in fact, the essence of beauty, but not the harmony of principally unlike elements, not the resolution of clashing contrasts in a complexity of artistic tensions, but, rather, the harmony of elements so alike and suited to one another that no harmonization would seem to be called for in the first place. Thus, the leading German theorist of taste, Johann Ulrich König, clarifies the issue in accordance with his French predecessors when he says that taste would approve of an object "which, after an exact examination of all its parts in themselves and their homogeneity, would deserve the approval of reason." [21] Needless to add, tragicomedy would seem to have the blessing of neither.

And yet it did, for face to face with the greatness of Shakespeare, the voice of taste was frequently silenced by that involuntary admiration which greatness commands, no matter in how unconventional or irregular a form it may appear.

The most telling example of this kind of unwilled, yet irresistible admiration can be seen in Voltaire's evaluation of Shakespeare in his *Lettres philosophiques* of 1734, first published the year before in English as *Letters Concerning the English Nation*. Voltaire is by no means a Shakespeare fan. Shakespeare, to him, did not have as much as "the least glimmer of taste," and one of the prime examples of this deficiency is his mingling of buffoonery with tragic horror and sublimity in his serious plays, as, for instance, in the gravedigger scene in *Hamlet* and the joking of the Roman cobblers in *Julius Caesar*, which, by the way, also aroused the ire of

Gottsched at about the same time.[22] But, unlike Gottsched, Voltaire is uncommitted enough to applaud, if *contre coeur*, the beauty this imperfection occasionally creates. Imperfection, while remaining imperfection, paradoxically assumes the features of a unique kind of perfection. The beauties are "irregular beauties," but beauties nonetheless. Or to put it the other way round: the monstrosities are monstrosities, but brilliant ones. Thus, Voltaire maintains in the final paragraph of the eighteenth "Letter" (from which the previous quotations were taken as well): "The brilliant monsters of Shakespeare are a thousand times more delightful than the sagacity of the moderns. The poetic genius of the English until now has resembled a thick-spreading tree planted by nature, lifting its thousand branches as it pleases, and growing irregularly and with vigor. Prune it against its nature to the shape of a tree in the gardens of Marly, and it will die." [23] There is a similar stealthy admiration for the irregular beauties of Shakespeare in the young Johann Elias Schlegel's comparison (1741) of Shakespeare and Andreas Gryphius,[24] in John Upton's *Critical Observations on Shakespeare* (1746, p. 107), and in Mrs. Montagu's *Essay on the Writings and Genius of Shakespeare* (1769, p. 101). Wieland, almost echoing Voltaire, coins a memorable phrase in the conclusion of an essay on Shakespeare in the *Teutsche Merkur* in 1773 when he says that Shakespeare's "mistakes are themselves very often a kind of beauty." [25] This is precisely the point.

Such admiration, to be sure, can be suppressed, and it was, and not necessarily by lesser minds, though, as elsewhere, these were more successful at this dubious manoeuvre. It might, therefore, be worthwhile to throw the positive appreciation of the mingling of kings and clowns into relief by concentrating first on the more conservative, negative evaluations. In this way, our glimpse of this phase of the history of taste may become more meaningful.

In France, perhaps the most influential exponent of the orthodox neoclassical view was Abbé d'Aubignac in his *Pratique du Théâtre* (1657). Not only did he condemn the juxtaposition and succession of the "tragic" and the "comic" in the popular *Théâtre Italien* as evidence of bad taste in the sense we discussed above, but he even went so far as to deny the legitimacy of the designation tragicomedy to tragedy with a happy ending (which usually also intermixed some "comic stuff"). He argued that since the subtitle of such a play signaled the happy resolution of whatever tragic complications were presented, the audience would not even be able to appreciate the "tragic" as tragic but as a transitional phenomenon which, as such, could not be taken seriously. Thus, *tragi*comedy would never get off the ground.[26] This reflection of Aubignac is somewhat on the periphery of our discussion, but it nonetheless deserves to be mentioned. Joseph Addison, by the way, was to attack the "chimerical notion" of poetic justice as a device taken for granted in the tragedy of his time by a very similar if not identical line of argument (*Spectator*, No. 40, 1711).

With Milton's preface to *Samson Agonistes* (1671), however, we are again in the mainstream of our argument. Milton claims that he endeavors "to vindicate tragedy from the small esteem, or rather infamy, which in the account of many it undergoes at this day, with other common interludes; happening through the poet's error of intermixing comic stuff with tragic sadness and gravity, or introducing trivial and vulgar persons; which by all judicious hath been counted absurd and brought in without discretion, corruptly to gratify the people." Gottsched in Germany at the beginning of the eighteenth century—his *Critische Dichtkunst* was published in 1730—was still of the same opinion, and as the literary dictator of his country he was in a position to make it stick while blandly accusing any possible dissenters in advance as "ignorant" (p. 17). Friedrich Nicolai in his

Briefe über den itzigen Zustand der schönen Wissen-
schaften in Deutschland (*Letters on the Present State of*
the Liberal Arts in Germany, 1755) even felt the need
to apologize, in this context, for the German national
character (Ninth Letter). National character, he felt,
was best expressed in plays, and the fact was that, even
then, irregular, mixed dramas dominated the stage in
Germany, as they did elsewhere. Flatteringly enough,
this left-handed denigration proved unintentionally that
Germans were good Europeans (while Frederick the
Great, less graciously, though intentionally, opined in
his *De la littérature allemande,* 1780, that the mongrel
productions of the Germans were worthy rather of the
savages of Canada).

Diderot in the third "Entretien" on his *Fils Naturel*
(1757) had much the same complaint to make as Milton
and Nicolai: "Tragicomedy can only be a bad kind, because in it one mingles two kinds remote from each
other and separated by a natural barrier. One does not
pass from the one to the other by imperceptible nuances. One is thrown into contrasts all the time, and
unity disappears. You see that this kind of play, in
which the most amusing features of comedy are placed
side by side with the most moving features of the serious genre and in which one always jumps from one
genre to the other, will not be without censure in the
eyes of a strict critic." [27] In other words, a literary genre
is the more perfect the more exclusively it relies for its
own effect on those means that are germane to itself. To
quote Karl Wilhelm Ramler: "a work which trans-
gresses the frontiers of a specific genre is so far from
achieving the highest idea of perfection that it begins,
on the contrary, to become a mistake." [28]

These critics have, like Chassiron, Rapin, James
Ralph, Edward Phillips, Thomas Rymer, John Dennis,
Weisse and others mentioned above, a pronounced, classical awareness of the purity of comedy and tragedy
alike. But it never seems to have occurred to them that

the specific effects of tragedy, for example, could be accomplished—perhaps in a superior fashion—by the use of means supposedly proper in comedy alone, that the tragic might be heightened by the comic if it were interspersed judiciously. Walpole suggested this in the preface to *The Castle of Otranto*, published in 1764. Friedrich Schlegel, not to mention his more scholarly methodical brother August Wilhelm, pointed out similar complex effects in Shakespearean plays to his German readers while Francisque Sarcey in his *Essai d'une esthétique du théâtre* (*A Theory of the Theater*, 1876) limited the function of the comic in tragedy to precisely this heightening of the single, tragic effect. Somehow, the conservative neoclassicists failed to appreciate such effects even when these are most impressively accomplished. Christoph Martin Wieland's commentaries to his Shakespeare translation are a case in point.[29] Although he was much more liberal on other occasions, the comic incidents strewn into Shakespeare's tragedies and histories are, for him, mere evidence of "bedlam taste" and of subservience to the wishes of a crude audience, who expected a hearty laugh for their sixpence. The early Johann Elias Schlegel in his essay comparing Shakespeare and Andreas Gryphius (1741) and F. Nicolai in his *Treatise on Tragedy* (1755) specifically ruled out comic incidents in tragedy because they would not arouse those emotions appropriate to tragedy. In other words, it was felt and, in fact, taken for granted that the means would have to correspond in kind to the desired end. Even the principle of imitation of nature, both Schlegel and Nicolai asserted, did not provide an excuse for inserting comic incidents.[30]

The idea underlying this failure to understand certain Shakespearean examples of what we would consider perfect integration of the comic into the overall tragic effect must have been the conviction that conflicting emotions, when placed close together, are not only unpleasant, as Henry Home had stated, but would also weaken each other and thereby detract from the intended results. "In a word," Richard Hurd says in his *Dissertation on the Provinces of Drama* (1753), "though *mixed dramas* may give us pleasure, yet the pleasure . . . will be less in proportion to the mixture. And the *end* of each will be then attained most perfectly when its character, according to the ancient practice, is observed." [31] Dryden, though he had defended the hybrids of the native tradition which he himself produced en masse, in his *Essay of Dramatic Poesy* of 1668, made this point even more incisively toward the end of his life in *A Parallel of Poetry and Painting* (1695):

The Gothic manner, and the barbarous ornaments, which are to be avoided in a picture, are just the same with those in an ill-ordered play. For example, our English tragi-comedy must be confessed to be wholly Gothic, notwithstanding the success which it has found upon our theatre, and in the *Pastor Fido* of Guarini; even though Corisca and the Satyr contribute somewhat to the main action. Neither can I defend my *Spanish Friar*, as fond as otherwise I am of it, from this imputation: for though the comical parts are diverting, and the serious moving, yet they are of an unnatural mingle: for mirth and gravity destroy each other, and are no more to be allowed for decent than a gay widow laughing in a mourning habit.[32]

And Addison, though not actually referring to Dryden, seems to continue the argument a few years later (1711) in the *Spectator* (No. 40) where he states categorically: "the tragi-comedy, which is the product of the English theater, is one of the most monstrous inventions that ever entered into a poet's thoughts. An author might as well think of weaving the adventures of Aeneas and Hudibras into one poem, as of writing such a motley piece of mirth and sorrow. But the absurdity of these performances is so very visible that I shall not insist upon it." One could easily cite a good many similar neo-classical denunciations of tragicomedy as a "barbaric," "gothic" "monstrosity." These key words occur again

and again with suspicious regularity wherever one looks
in European criticism of the time. Even Madame de
Staël strikes this note in her famous *De la littérature
considerée dans ses rapports avec les institutions sociales*
(1800) when she contends that even Shakespeare's manner of having comic scenes follow "tragic effects" is
"bizarre" and makes "a disagreeable impression on men
of taste." [33] And the psycho-aesthetic reason for the re-
jection of the matching of hornpipes and funerals in
drama that Dryden had formulated in 1695 is repeated,
for instance, in Spain, in Ignacio de Luzán's French-in-
spired compendium of neoclassical rules, *La Poética o
reglas de la poesía* (1737):

> To mingle kings and princes with lowly people, and dole-
> ful events with jocose jests, the tragic with the comic, is to
> spoil the one as well as the other. For, while on the one hand
> the comical remarks interrupt the force of the tragic emo-
> tions of sorrow and terror inopportunely, on the other hand,
> the deaths and dismal events and the solemn gravity of the
> tragic persons, cool off and disturb the most lively comic
> mirth, and finally, in one's endeavor to enjoy all the ends of
> tragedy and comedy together, one enjoys none, and the audi-
> ence neither laughs right nor weeps right; and although it
> laughs and weeps, it equally spoils its mourning and its
> laughter, as the one disconcerts and destroys all the good ef-
> fects of the other, and vice versa.[34]

Finally, this judgment of neoclassicist taste and reason is
reiterated as late as 1820 by Alessandro Manzoni who,
"comme un bon et loyal partisan du classique," asserts in
his *Lettre à Mr. C* [Victor Chauvet] that the "mélange
de deux effets contraires" "destroys the unity of impression which is necessary to produce emotion and sympathy." [35]

No clairvoyance is required to see that such views
stem directly from the notion of "good taste" as it was
expounded at the time. And yet the voice of good taste,
or taste anyway, could be made to speak in a very
different tone in the same period, indeed in the critical

work of one and the same man. Dryden when he
claimed in 1695 that "mirth and gravity destroy each
other" was actually quoting and reversing a statement
he had made in the *Essay of Dramatic Poesy* in the guise
of Neander who refuted Lisideius' assertion that the
"mixture of comedy and tragedy" in the native *drame
libre* was barbarically "absurd" and "unnatural." Neander contended that he had to "have stronger arguments,
ere I am convinced that compassion and mirth in the
same subject destroy each other," and even added, in
curious counterpoint to Nicolai's later national concern,
that in the meantime he could not "but conclude, to the
honor of our nation, that we have invented, increased,
and perfected a more pleasant way of writing for the
stage than was ever known to the ancients or moderns
of any nation, which is tragi-comedy." [36]

Tragicomedy, though rejected by the orthodox as unnatural, is vindicated as "natural" by Neander-Dryden.
As Dr. Johnson was to say later, in his *Preface to
Shakespeare* (1768): "there is always an appeal open
from criticism to nature." Now, "nature," though Johnson does not say so, could mean one of two things: the
nature of reality as seen and interpreted by reasonable
taste, or the nature of our psycho-aesthetic response as
seen and interpreted by reasonable taste. Dryden chose
the second course of appeal when he had Neander argue:

As for their new way of mingling mirth with serious plot,
I do not, with Lisideius, condemn the thing, though I cannot
approve their manner of doing it. He tells us, we cannot so
speedily recollect ourselves after a scene of great passion and
concernment, as to pass to another of mirth and humor, and
to enjoy it with any relish: but why should he imagine the
soul of man more heavy than his senses? Does not the eye
pass from an unpleasant object to a pleasant in a much
shorter time than is required to this? and does not the un-
pleasantness of the first commend the beauty of the latter?
The old rule of logic might have convinced him, that contraries, when placed near, set off each other. A continued

gravity keeps the spirit too much bent; we must refresh it
sometimes, as we bait in a journey that we may go on with
greater ease. A scene of mirth, mixed with tragedy, has the
same effect upon us which our music has betwixt the acts;
which we find a relief to us from the best plots and language
of the stage, if the discourses have been long.[37]

One must forego charity in interpreting this passage,
for it is by no means entirely clear just how Dryden
wants us to understand the function of the comic interspersed with the tragic. It *is* clear that he maintains that
the contraries do not cancel each other out. But does he
mean that the contraries "set off *each other*," or does he
imply that the comic incidents merely serve to
strengthen our appreciation of the tragic as tragic while
a corresponding vice versa relation is not to be counted
on? Judging by this crucial passage, one feels that the
latter alternative is by far the more probable one. Dryden hardly follows up the notion, which seems to be
there rudimentarily, that the psycho-aesthetic relation
between the comic and the tragic might be a *mutual*
one. Only such a mutual relation, however, would result
in the tragicomic in the modern sense of the word. In the
last analysis, then, Dryden values the comic-relief elements as means in tragedy of heightening its own, tragic
effect. This clarification does, however, not detract
from the merit of his view. His exposition is certainly
significant in the history of literary taste as the first step
taken towards an appreciation of the more complete and
subtle mingling of the tragic and the comic. As early as
1668 Dryden formulates a principle of the interaction of
the tragic and the comic which, as was already pointed
out, did not really gain acceptance until the Romantics
and their Shakespeare criticism while the more conservative neoclassicists, even Wieland, especially in their
criticism of the "comic relief" in Shakespeare's tragedies
and histories, failed to see the point.

Dryden, then, came very close to a description of the
tragicomic, for while he failed to go into the possibility

of the reciprocity of the interaction of the comic and
the tragic, he must surely have been aware that the
comic means, when it functioned to achieve a tragic
end, remained a comic one and was not totally absorbed
in the overall effect. Clearly, the tragicomic could be
approached from this avenue, that is, from an examination of the nature of our aesthetic sensibility vis-à-vis
literary works. And it was approached from this avenue.
But before such time, in the eighteenth century, the
other possible avenue was explored, that is to say: an
appeal was made from criticism to the "nature" of outward reality.

This was in fact the way of Dr. Johnson, who had
spoken of this recourse to "nature" from "criticism."
Discussing "tragicomedy" (which his *Dictionary* defined as "drama compounded of merry and serious
events") in No. 156 of *The Rambler* in 1751, he ex-
claimed:

> For what is there in the mingled drama which impartial
> reason can condemn? The connection of important with
> trivial incidents, since it is not only common but perpetual
> in the world, may surely be allowed upon the stage, which
> pretends only to be the mirror of life. . . . Is it not certain
> that the tragic and comic affections have been moved al-
> ternately with equal force, and that no plays have oftener
> filled the eye with tears, and the breast with palpitation, than
> those which are variegated with interludes of mirth? . . . It
> ought to be the first endeavor of a writer to distinguish na-
> ture from custom; or that which is established because it is
> right, from that which is right only because it is established;
> that he may neither violate essential principles by a desire of
> novelty, nor debar himself from the attainment of beauties
> within his view, by a needless fear of breaking rules which
> no literary dictator had authority to enact.

Reason, which more commonly defined "nature" as
beautiful in the sense of harmony of homogeneous elements, is here called upon to justify the mixture of the
comic and the tragic as corresponding to "nature"
which the drama is to reflect. This, however, was noth-

ing new. Sixteenth-century critics like Macropedius, Cinthio, and Guarini had tried a similar apology for mixed dramas by recourse to an equally generously interpreted "nature." Lope de Vega did the same ("buen exemplo nos da naturaleza") in his *Arte Nuevo de Hacer Comedias en este Tiempo* (1609) although it should be pointed out that this defense in an after-dinner speech is nowadays no longer taken quite seriously as a formulation of Lope's views on the stage. But François Ogier had definitely been serious in his preface to Jean de Schelandre's "tragicomédie" *Tyr et Sidon* (1628) where he defended the current practice of mingling mirth and sorrow by an appeal to the same reason and nature that Johnson was to speak of:

This plan of ordering and arranging, which they [the ancients] used, is our reason for not hesitating to justify the invention of tragi-comedies, introduced by the Italians, in view of the fact that it is much more reasonable, in the course of the same conversation, to mingle grave matters with the least serious, and to bring them together in a single plot for a play or for a story, than to mingle extraneously satyrs with tragedies that have no connection with one another, and that confuse and disturb the sight and the understanding of the audience; for, to say that it is improper to show in a single play the same persons speaking now of serious, important, and tragic matters, and immediately after of commonplace, vain, and humorous things, is to be unacquainted with the nature of human life, whose days and hours are very often interrupted by laughter and by tears, by joy and by sorrow, according as they are filled with happiness or troubled by misfortune.[38]

In Germany, C. M. Wieland used the example of Shakespeare to make the same point. He was fascinated by the wealth of impressions offered by Shakespearean drama and annoyed by the contemporary criticism of Shakespeare's plays to the effect

that the comic and the tragic are jumbled together in them in the strangest manner and that frequently one and the same person, who through the moving language of nature has

made us cry, a few moments later, by some strange idea or
baroque expression of his feelings, if he does not actually
make us laugh, cools us off to such a degree that it becomes
hard to regain our proper frame of mind. People criticize
this—and do not think of it that his plays are for this very
reason all the more natural portraits of human life.

But when making this emphatic statement in his famous and popular novel *Agathon* in 1767,[39] Wieland actually went a significant step further than the other critics quoted in this context. While they merely justified
the juxtaposition and succession of the comic and the
tragic by an appeal to nature, Wieland, moreover, conceived of at least one type of coordination or even integration of the tragic and the comic which results in the
complex phenomenon that we call the tragicomic. In the
continuation of his argument, he remarks that in the
drame libre of the popular tradition (*Haupt- und Staats-
aktionen*) which he calls tragicomedy, the clown ordinarily played a significant part, but not only in such
plays, but also in the tragicomedy of life:

But how many great acts have been performed on the
stage of the world at all times with the clown, or what is a
little worse, by the clown? How often have the greatest men,
born to be the protective spirits of a throne, the benefactors
of entire peoples and ages, seen all their wisdom and bravery
foiled by a small whimsical prank of the clown or such people who while not wearing his coat and yellow trousers certainly had his entire character? How often is it that in both
tragicomedies, the very complication stems from nothing but
the fact that all of a sudden the clown ruins the endeavors
of the wise people by some stupid and roguish example of
his work?

What Wieland perceives here is the possibility of a
rather crude kind of integration of the comic into the
tragic: a comic agent brings about a tragic effect. If
both, comic agent and tragic effect, are not separated
from each other by too much interrupting material, if,
moreover, both appear within the same scene, side by
side, in interaction, the tragicomic, the identity of the

comic and the tragic, might indeed result. Christian
Weise had already approached such a "tragicomedy"
that integrated the tragic and the comic in this fashion
in his *Masaniello* (1683)[40] where a comical tyrant causes
a fair amount of tragic suffering. And later Hebbel was
to develop this kind of integration theoretically. Indeed,
his theory of tragicomedy gained wide acceptance in
Germany around the turn of the century.

But let us return to the principle of imitation of nature. Wieland's example shows that it was possible to
arrive from this premise not only at an "additive" variety of tragicomedy, but also at "synthetic" tragicomedy, that is, a play which is largely comic and tragic at
the same time. Only a very crude type of synthetic tragicomedy would, however, seem possible from this starting point—crude because of the crassly clashing nature
of the contrast of the tragic and the comic rather than
a subtle blend of the two which nonetheless leaves each
intact and unweakened.

A more subtle kind of tragicomic integration might,
on the other hand, be conceived of from the other
approach, that is, from concentration on the nature of
our aesthetic sensibility rather than on the nature of
reality. The decisive initial step, we recall, had been
taken by Dryden. The final step was taken by Gotthold
Ephraim Lessing oddly enough within months after
Wieland had chanced upon tragicomic integration from
a diametrically opposite starting point. In an amateurish
way, Lessing's position was anticipated, however, by a
young critic whom scholars have accorded increasingly
more serious attention as a pioneer and fore-runner:
Johann Elias Schlegel.

His secret fascination, at an early date, with what
Voltaire called the irregular beauties of Shakespeare's
plays has already been mentioned—as well as his *theoretical* reservations about the mixture of the tragic and
the comic. Schlegel really comes into his own, however,
with a later work, the *Gedanken zur Aufnahme des*

dänischen Theaters (*Thoughts on the Betterment of the Danish Theater*, 1747). In this treatise Schlegel sketches a typology of drama. Five basic types of plays are envisioned: dramas of noble persons which arouse the passions, dramas of noble persons which arouse laughter, dramas of lowly persons which arouse the passions, dramas of lowly persons which arouse laughter, and finally "actions of noble or lowly persons or a mixed cast (*vermischte Personen*) which arouse partly the passions, partly laughter." Obviously, this fifth kind is of the greatest interest in the present context. Schlegel does not call it tragicomedy, but, then, his designations are irritatingly one-sided; he calls only the first type tragedy, all the others comedy, using to all appearances quite arbitrarily both the criterion of the social class of the *dramatis personae* and that of the types of effects aroused by the drama. But no matter, in contemporaneous usage the fifth type would have been called tragicomedy. More important than terminology, of course, is the way Schlegel views the combination of the effects proper to tragedy and those proper to comedy in his fifth type of drama. Tragedy, that is, a play designed to arouse our passions, is to exclude every hint of the ridiculous. Yet, on the other hand, comedy, that is, a play designed to arouse laughter, is by no means bound to banish the passions from its domain; on the contrary, "in most cases" they are not only advantageous, but "almost necessary." But is this merely a defense of the *juxtaposition* of kings and clowns, hornpipes and funerals? Clearly not. For a few pages further on, Schlegel remarks that the most important factor in the success of a play is the sympathy of the audience with a figure on the stage, with whom it suffers and with whom it sympathizes. Schlegel concludes that even laughter would have to be "mingled with the excitement of some passions." This "mingling" cannot be an additive principle. Schlegel comes to the point when he says: "At times the ridiculous is fused with the passions to such an extent that both are aroused at the same time. An example of this may be seen when the cash-box of Molière's miser is taken away from him. At this point, the poor wretch arouses pity and laughter at the same time. Molière was generally an incomparable master of this art, and Arnolf in *The School for Wives*, when he is desperately in love, is another example of it." [41]

The comic is identical with the tragic in these instances that Schlegel points out in this remarkable anticipation of more modern Molière interpretations. What he talks about is no longer a succession or juxtaposition of the emotions aroused by the comic and the tragic but an indissoluble fusion of the two in such a way that they do not weaken each other, but rather throw light upon each other and, thereby, even intensify each other. Typical for his time, Schlegel proceeds from the *effect* of a literary work on the reader or viewer; but he is the first to realize that a synthetically tragicomic effect is possible. This is indeed a remarkable position to take even for an ambitious young critic, for the consensus at the time was that such a mixed reaction was patently impossible. Two years after Schlegel's essay, Chassiron, though not referring to the German critic, states this view with the categorical casualness that befits the expression of a truism (*Réflexions sur le comique-larmoyant*, 1749), throwing into relief Schlegel's daring formulation and its significance in the history of taste in the eighteenth century.

Schlegel died too young to establish himself as a major critic. But his view on tragicomic integration found a national and, in fact, international voice when Lessing, in his prestigious *Hamburgische Dramaturgie* (1767-1769), propounded it with both stimulating suggestivity and authority. He did not, to be sure, refer to J.E. Schlegel, whom scholars have regarded as his "predecessor" in many respects; but the similarity of his position and approach is striking. Lessing, too, has nothing but contempt for the idea that the mixtures and contrasts of

multifarious "nature" are a valid precedent for the mingling of kings and clowns and the matching of hornpipes and funerals in drama. He even resorts to the time-
honored terms "gothic" and "barbaric" in referring to
the results of this error of judgment (Section 70). But
while the "nature" of the phenomenal world is no excuse for mixed drama, he continues, "the nature of our
sensations and psychic abilities" (*Seelenkräfte*) certainly is. And again, what this critic has in mind is not
the succession and juxtaposition of the tragic and the
comic but an integration which makes the tragic appear
in comic guise, and the comic in tragic guise. Thus,
Lessing remarks, quite abruptly and without drawing
further conclusions, that the impossible is possible:
"only if this event in its progress assumes all shades of
interest and one does not merely follow upon the other,
but of necessity evolves from it, if gravity provokes
laughter, sadness pleasure or vice versa, so directly that
an abstraction of the one or the other is impossible to us,
then only do we not demand it from art and art knows
how to draw a profit from this impossibility." [42]

What Lessing describes in this isolated passage has
nothing to do with the *comédie larmoyante* at which
he himself had tried his hand. What he describes is indeed the phenomenon of the tragicomic, for what he
means by his somewhat vague designation of the mixed
emotional responses to drama are, as the context makes
incontrovertibly clear, the emotions aroused by tragedy
on the one hand and comedy on the other. It is these
that are to be fused inextricably.

It is not too much to say that the endeavors of European critics throughout the neoclassical age, since the
second half of the seventeenth century, reach their climax in this formulation of Lessing. His expression "impossibility" in describing the complex response to the
synthetically tragicomic is indeed telling: what traditional aesthetics and psychology had deemed impossible,
Lessing daringly claims to be possible.

To sum up: it cannot be said, as it has been, that neo-classicism contributed nothing towards an appreciation of tragicomic drama and condemned it outright. The fact is, as our examples have indicated, that neoclassicist critics not only defended the succession and juxtaposition of the comic and the tragic on aesthetic and psychological grounds, but they also conceived of the possibility of a fusion of the two. This fusion, far from weakening the tragic and comic, strengthened each in a precarious, though thinkable union which, while preserving the identity of each, made each identical with the other. This appreciation was reached from both possible avenues of approach: from a consideration of the "nature" of outward reality, on the one hand, and from a study of the "nature" of our aesthetic sensibilities, on the other. Both avenues have in common that their milestones are those of what was then called "good taste." It is no coincidence that the essential statements on this point were made around the middle of the eighteenth century and shortly thereafter, for here is the main divide between traditional and what, for want of a better term, has been called modern literary criticism.

It is at this crucial point in the development of European aesthetics and criticism that Johann Elias Schlegel's brother Johann Adolf, in his appendix to his translation (1751) of Batteux' *Les beaux arts*, remarked: "I believe that the question is whether the eye which views an object is happy or melancholy, capricious or gentle. This difference can, at times, make even the same objects, shown from the same point of view in the same manner, so different that entirely different genres are the result, each requiring its own rules" (p. 310). As if in reply to this general question, which cast grave doubt on the traditional view that subject matter determines the genre of a play, Lessing stated less than a generation later that it was not beyond human aesthetic sensibilities to view one and the same object in diametrically opposed moods at one and the same time; Lessing asserted that one could

in fact, to retain the image that Johann Adolf Schlegel
had used, view an event on stage with one weeping and
one laughing eye. Johann Adolf's brother had pointed
to Molière's *L'avare* and *L'école des Femmes* as examples of such double vision. It remains to be seen how
this double vision has gained ground since the late
eighteenth century.

Yet, before one plunges into an examination of the
history of the appreciation of the tragicomic, it would
be wise to bear in mind that the definition of the tragicomic and tragicomedy that we have thus far gained,
guided as we were by the critical appraisals of neoclassicist critics, is still vague, and, moreover, superficial. None
of the critics discussed really goes beyond the description
of the tragicomic and a more or less enthusiastic preference for it. Following them, we have approached
what tragicomedy can mean in modern times, but we
are still far from understanding its nature with any
subtlety of appreciation. This, however, can only be
achieved by way of an examination of some of the problems inherent in any discussion of modern tragicomedy.
These problems emerge as the "successors" of the eighteenth-century pioneers turn to the genre. They will be
discussed in the next chapter.

CHAPTER

II

Theory of Tragicomedy

---

*"Things have different qualities,
and the soul has different inclinations, for nothing that offers itself to the soul is simple
and the soul never offers itself
to anything simply. Hence one
weeps and laughs about the same
thing."*

BLAISE PASCAL,
Pensées, No. 112
(Edition Brunschvicg)

The Identity of Opposites

The definition of tragicomedy tentatively suggested at
the end of Chapter I is predicated on the assumption
that it is conceivable for an audience to be able to perceive and experience the comic and the tragic qualities
of a given event, situation, or character simultaneously
without detriment to either. It further assumes that the
dramatist approached his subject matter with this double
vision and molded it in his play in such a way that a
corresponding reaction was evoked on the part of the
audience. This is what modern writers and critics like
Luigi Pirandello, Eugène Ionesco, Friedrich Dürrenmatt, Jack Richardson, and Harold Pinter presuppose
when they discuss the intricate fusion of comedy and

tragedy in some of their own dramas, which they may or may not call tragicomedies. Ionesco goes so far as to profess that he "never understood the difference people make between the comic and the tragic," adding that he is convinced "that the comic is tragic" and vice versa.[1]

This identification of opposites, which is basic to tragicomedy, does, however, involve a number of problems. First of all, it is not always clear just what these authors mean by "the comic" and "the tragic." And even if it is, their notions of these phenomena are hardly the same. To be sure, they no longer talk, as did their predecessors in the seventeenth century, in terms of such component elements as style, *dramatis personae*, motifs, and conclusion, from which a composite genre, "tragicomedy," could formerly be so easily constructed. But this is faint consolation, for a cynic might point out that there are at least as many theories of comedy and of tragedy as there are critics. Still, some basic patterns do emerge. These, however, do not necessarily suggest support for the modern notion that the comic and the tragic are compatible or even identical. On the contrary, they also tend to support the belief that they are fundamentally incongruent. Let us look at three such frequently held ideas.

Particularly disturbing in its popularity is the time-honored idea that comedy appeals to the intellect while tragedy engages the feelings. Horace Walpole's aphorism that life is a comedy to those who think and a tragedy to those who feel, makes its appearance with disconcerting regularity in many contemporary dramatic theories. Of this contrast one could also speak in terms of detachment or distance, on the one hand, and identification or empathy, on the other. And more likely than not, one would be tempted to conclude, as Henri Bergson did in his famous and influential essay on laughter (*Le Rire*, 1900) that laughter, or let us say, perception of the comic, is incompatible with emotional participa-

tion. One would be tempted to agree with Ronald Peacock's seemingly level-headed reminder: "In the midst
of more intricate details of aesthetic analysis it is well to
state a simple truth: drama must be one of two things:
either comic or intensely moving." [2] But some tempta-
tions are really productive provocations, and this is one
of them, for quite apart from the fact that one cannot
separate emotional and mental reactions quite so accurately, is not the appreciation of the tragedy of Oedipus
heightened by the ineluctable perception of the irony
that pervades the development of his situation and
"fate"? This irony, it is true, is experienced in an attitude of aesthetic detachment, which is perhaps more
familiar in comedy; but is not its ultimate as well as immediate effect an even deeper emotional awareness of
the tragic? And vice versa, is not the appreciation of the
comic, predominantly intellectual as it may be, increased and enriched by a certain degree of emotional
involvement which may even induce us to laugh at ourselves as we laugh at the *dramatis personae*, knowingly
and all the more sympathetically as, for instance, in
Hofmannsthal's *Der Schwierige* (*The Difficult Man*)?
There are, to be sure, the slick Broadway musicals, the
mordant satires, the Restoration comedies, and the farcical spoofs which one and all do not permit any amount
of empathy. But these are clearly on the edge of the
mainstream of European and American drama. The more
standard play, if neither "epic" nor "absurd," depends
for its effect on a more or less subtle union: in the attitude of the audience, of sympathetic participation and
emotional involvement, on the one hand, and aesthetic
distance and intellectual awareness, on the other.[3] This
union, it will be seen, is also the *sine qua non* of tragicomedy, indeed, the basis of its possibility—with this
distinction, however, that here, and only here, the opposites, which are experienced simultaneously rather than
alternately, are equally strong.

Another antithesis between comedy and tragedy

which one encounters frequently in dramatic theory is
equally fallacious. At first glance it would seem to make
it hard to admit, on theoretical grounds, the fusion of
the tragic and the comic. It states that the tragic is a
quality inherent in life or the human condition as such,
that, hence, it is something objective, whereas the comic
would invariably be a matter of subjective perception
which "makes" something comical by a particular way
of viewing it. Yet both of these complementary assumptions invite doubt and contrary formulations. For one
thing, whether one views life, the world, and the human
condition as tragic per se is a matter of *Weltanschauung*
and consequently open to equally subjective challenges;
Aristophanes and some Romanticists would prefer to
think that life is rather a comedy and Walpole would
add that this is every thinking man's view. But, more
seriously, is one not forced to assume that even the
comic is to a certain extent an objective quality of life?
Must not the school of thought that considers the
comic as a matter of perception only admit that it is
merely certain "objective" facts and relations, proportions or disproportions in reality that encourage or
elicit the comic perception while others do not? That
everything lends itself to comic perception is a proposi-
tion that is difficult to maintain. A recent film, a latter-
day *Candide*, proves this point involuntarily by its unsuccessful attempt to show the world of concentration
camps in the light of comedy, bitter comedy, but comedy nonetheless.

As for the other half of the theory under discussion
(that the tragic is a quality of life), it has frequently
been pointed out that the tragic is equally dependent
upon the viewer's manner of perception as is the comic.
Friedrich Schiller put it in a nutshell when he said:
"What makes the subject matter tragic or comic is not
the realm from which it was taken, but the forum before which the poet brings it." [4] Similarly, Francisque
Sarcey observed in his *Essai d'une esthétique du théâtre*

(1876): "In themselves, events are not cheerful and they are not sad. They are neither. It is we who impregnate them with our sentiment or color them to our liking. An old man falls; the street urchin who is passing holds his sides and laughs. The woman cries out with pity. It is the same event; but the one has thought only of the ridiculousness of the fall, the other has seen only the danger. The second wept where the first found cause only for laughter." [5] Hence the divergent ways in which one and the same motif can be treated in literature.

If, then, both the tragic and the comic may be a matter of objective reality as well as of subjective perception, it is thinkable, not only that certain proportions of reality "are" comic and tragic at the same time, but, more significantly, that they can be *seen* that way, with one weeping and one laughing eye. This was one of the feats of "the weeping and laughing Jean of the legend," as Sarcey reminds us.[6] Yet, surely, one does not need the purification of a martyr to react this way, helpful though it may be.

A third stumbling block in our way to a theory of the synthetically tragicomic genre is not quite so judiciously placed and is overcome more easily. The world of comedy, it is frequently asserted, is limited to the realm of immanence, while tragedy is open to transcendence. Neither part of this antithesis is tenable, unless one capriciously narrows one's concept of one or both genres to specific historical types. That tragedy can dispense entirely with metaphysical vistas has been demonstrated by Eugene O'Neill and a host of others; in fact, in *Mourning Becomes Electra* the idea of transcendental fate has been consistently and intentionally replaced by those causative factors of tragedy which are on the purely human and social level, heredity and environment. That comedy, on the other hand, is quite capable of treating the relation of man to the universe and indeed his fate in a metaphysical sense of the word,

is not a particularly recent idea. It is suggested in Plato's
Laws where the Athenian embarks on the philosophical
venture of proving that the meaning of human life is
that humans are the playthings of the gods (644 d).
"Metaphysical comedy" is precisely what German Romanticism aims at (but never quite achieves), and the
"metaphysical farce" is a distinctive genre of our time.
Moreover, no clairvoyance is necessary to understand
that such a drama will easily tend to become tragicomic
rather than "purely" comic since the cynical notion of a
comically perverted religiosity can hardly be sustained
for any length of time. It is no coincidence that one of
the most vociferous advocates of tragicomedy in our
time, Ionesco, jotted down in his diary the suspicion
concerning the contradictions in the world: "is it a god
making fun of man?" [7] What is meant by metaphysical
tragicomedy or metaphysical comedy can best be illus-
trated by a glance at *King Lear*, which, as G. Wilson
Knight has shown in *The Wheel of Fire*, incorporates a
good deal of comedy of the metaphysical variety. Lear
is the "fool of fortune" (IV, vi, 185); and though
Gloucester's famous remark "As flies are to wanton boys
are we to the Gods:/they kill us for their sport" (IV, i,
37-38) is certainly not the key to the drama as a whole,
there are moments in the play where this couplet comes
to mind with powerful suggestivity. Instead of throwing
incense on "such sacrifices" (V, iii, 20) the Gods laugh
at a farce instituted by themselves. We, the audience,
may join in this Olympic laughter, but it will inevitably
assume a tragic ring as we realize the human suffering
and futility that is its price.

After we have cleared away these stumbling blocks of
dramatic theory, we have, in fact, begun to pave the
way for a theoretical demonstration of the chances and
possibilities of tragicomedy: Our discussion suggested
that the objections could be viewed as potential affirma-
tions, for in all three cases we were dealing with antitheses too neat to be real. Antitheses, however, possess

the virtue of pointing to something that the opposites have in common, as is true of all the other antithetical methods of defining comedy and tragedy. Without similarity there could be no difference, and all comparison would be doomed to failure from the outset. This is probably what Socrates had in mind when he threw out the suggestion that the genius of comedy was the same as that of tragedy. Thomas Mann continued this line of thought by specific reference to the *Symposium* when he has someone remark in *Doctor Faustus* (1947) that comedy and tragedy "grow on the same tree, and a change of lighting suffices to make one into the other." [8]

Yet precisely what is this "same tree," this similarity they both share? We must ask this question since the similarity of the two extreme genres, if reduced to its most basic proportion, is the key to an understanding of the theoretical possibility of identifying the comic and the tragic in modern tragicomedy. Without such a similarity it would be impossible to do what Ionesco, like many other modern dramatists, declares to be his endeavor: "to confront comedy and tragedy in order to link them in a new dramatic synthesis." [9] What, then, is the link?

There is no lack of answers. They are bound to be vague since a wide variety of plays will have to be accommodated by the formula. At the same time, they have to be specific enough to be applicable in a meaningful way. Whether or not they are found to be convincing depends very much on the nature and scope of the literary experience of the critic and reader. Logically, one could never amass enough plays to prove one's point; and if one selects so-called representative examples, there is, and rightly so, the same raising of eyebrows, for there are no standards of what is representative. Such is the nature of all abstractions. Bearing these difficulties in mind and rushing in where angels fear to tread, one could start with the following tentative and sufficiently flexible premise. *Conflict is the*

nerve of every drama, comic or tragic. The comic
"hero" as well as the tragic "hero" is in conflict with his
world, with some kind of order of his world which is
the accepted norm within the confines of the play.
What makes the comic or tragic hero unusual or outstanding is the fact that he is a misfit in his world.
Whether the order or overall framework of accepted
behavior or action in which he is a misfit is primarily a
social, religious, political or moral one, or a combination
of these, is not of major importance as long as the incongruity is poignantly brought out one way or another.
Nor is it of primary significance whether this order is
expressly formulated and represented within the play itself or (as is more often the case in comedy, especially
satiric comedy) it is presupposed on the part of the audience. Thus, a tragic hero may find himself at odds
with a world which he feels (unjustly and contrary to
the dictates of his own conscience) confines him by
a conventional religious or social framework: Antig-
one, Medea, Hamlet, Wallenstein. In a similar manner,
the comic "hero" deviates from the norm, going beyond
it or trying to dodge it. Hence the stock-in-trade of the
comic theater—the comedy of manners—depends for
its effect on the exaggeration of a particular character
trait beyond the dimensions prescribed by reasonable
convention: the miser, the vainglorious soldier, the boy-
crazy old spinster, the pedant.

In any event, the tension between the norm (or the
rule or ideal) and the individual who refuses to fit himself into it seems to lend itself equally well to comic and
tragic effects. Another formulation of the disparity
which is comic as well as tragic is proposed by Cyrus
Hoy. If it is not original, it certainly is stringent and
cogent:

What our argument comes to, then, is this: that in serious
drama, comic or tragic, we are confronted with what is, at
bottom, a single truth about the human condition. Man is
possessed of an ideal of human conduct, but circumstances

together with his own inherent failings conspire to make the belief that the ideal can be fulfilled a finally illusory one. But man persists in despite of all the odds, and in his persistence he may appear as nobly enduring, stubbornly unyielding, foolishly blind, or a combination of all three. The more forcibly and apparently these diverse qualities are linked in combination, the more surely sounds the note of tragicomedy.[10]

One may have reservations about the universality of this principle of comedy, tragedy, and tragicomedy, for quite apart from the fact that one may find it less than encouraging to think that there is to be just one single truth about the human condition, one wonders if this theory fits some standard cases that have a knack of coming to mind in a discussion of comedy and tragedy. Does the dichotomy described by Hoy and others add anything to our understanding of *Oedipus Rex?* Is it helpful for an appreciation of *King Lear* or *Hamlet?* Does Molière's miser (whom most critics take to be representative of a legion of comic heroes) have an ideal of human conduct that he fails to achieve? And so on. It seems that the interrelation of a character with his surrounding (what one would call action and what, as such, is the soul of virtually all drama) plays no real part in this view of the disparity common to all three genres. On the other hand, if one interprets the "ideal" to mean a standard which is not purely a matter of the particular character's conception and expectation of himself, one might subsume this formula under that common denominator suggested above.

Another pattern of incongruity equally susceptible of comic and tragic treatment that has been formulated recently as a key to the elusive interrelation of the two genres is that of the "incongruity between man and his destiny," or "the tension between human aspirations and the intractability of the world (or universal forces, or the gods, or destiny)." [11] This pattern is familiar in tragedy. It applies equally well to a large body of comedy, once allowances are made for the fact that, in comedy, "destiny" can not be much more than a euphemism for the course of events, and if the word is actually used in comedy, it is only tongue-in-cheek, with mock-seriousness. This, of course, makes it somewhat difficult to accept that critic's idea that there is any sort of parallelism and comparability between *Oedipus Rex* and *Tristram Shandy* even though E. M. Forster thought that the world of Sterne's comic novel was dominated by the god Muddle. Muddle and Moira are cousins too many times removed for comparison of family likeness. Even so, this theory, if one interprets "destiny" to mean something like the greater scheme of things or the total order prevalent in the play, could also be subsumed easily under the formula tentatively proposed earlier, namely the tension between the norm (or the rule or ideal or "world") and the individual who does not fit into it.

Be this as it may, there is no need at this point to establish with precision the details of such an all-encompassing formula. The essential thing to remember is that there is likely to be such a coordinating principle and that its outlines can be delineated with such terms as conflict, contradiction, incongruity, incompatibility, terms which do, of course, appear in most discussions of dramatic theory. If there were no such principle, it would be hard to understand why certain motifs (as distinguished from others), by virtue of an inherent structural predisposition, lend themselves particularly well to treatment in both genres or, in fact, all three. Sidney Howard considered his play on the theme of the January and May marriage, *They Knew What They Wanted*, a comic variation of O'Neill's tragedy *Desire under the Elms*. The misanthrope theme was treated (predominantly) tragically in Shakespeare's *Timon of Athens*, comically in Ferdinand Raimund's *Alpenkönig und Menschenfeind*, and tragicomically in Molière's *Misanthrope*. The Pyramus and Thisbe farce in *Mid-*

summer Night's Dream is, down to details, a comic, even parodistic version of *Romeo and Juliet*, much as Goethe's *Satyros* is a farcical counterpart to his *Prometheus* tragedy, or Strindberg's *Comrades* is a ludicrous transmogrification of *The Father*. It is no coincidence that writers are sometimes undecided as to whether they should deal with a motif in terms of comedy or tragedy (Cp. Schiller's reflections about the Warwick theme, letter to Goethe, August 20, 1799). It is easy to see that all of these plays are based, in a more or less obvious fashion, on some central incongruity between the protagonist and what we may call his "world." It is further obvious from these examples that it is possible to view this incongruity from the comic as well as from the tragic angle. Then, why should it not be possible to see it from both at the same time?

At this point one invariably encounters a standard objection. Kierkegaard phrased it most compactly in his *Concluding Unscientific Postscript:* "Wherever there is life, there is contradiction, and wherever there is contradiction, the comical is present. The tragic and the comic are the same, in so far as both are based on contradiction; but *the tragic is the suffering contradiction, the comical, the painless contradiction*." And a little farther on: "The comic apprehension evokes the contradiction or makes it manifest by having in mind the way out, which is why the contradiction is painless. The tragic apprehension sees the contradiction and despairs of a way out. . . . Wherever there exists a contradiction and the way out is not known, where the contradiction is not canceled and corrected in something higher, there the contradiction is not painless." [12] Simple as it is, there are two difficult assumptions underlying this statement. First, a modern writer like Ionesco can make a case for exactly the opposite idea, namely that the comic, being "an intuitive perception of the absurd," is "more hopeless than the 'tragic,'" adding significantly that "the 'comic' offers no escape." [13] Iones-

co's case is not entirely unconvincing in view of some
modern examples of extreme cosmic cynicism and pessimism. Secondly, and more importantly, the theory formulated by Kierkegaard might force us to assume that
the difference between tragedy and comedy is merely a
quantitative one, consisting in the amount of pain
caused by the same pattern of contradiction or incongruity in comedy and tragedy, respectively. This would
mean that "as regards the idea of incongruity, . . . the
major difference between [*Oedipus Rex* and *Tristram
Shandy*] is the amount of suffering involved." [14] Clearly,
if the similarity and dissimilarity of tragedy and comedy
were reducible to such quantitative proportions, the discussion would become banal and be, one fears, slightly
beside the point. Moreover, where are we then to draw
the line in regarding one play a comedy and another a
tragedy if we judge them by the "amount" of suffering
involved? And would tragicomedy then be defined as a
drama with a medium amount of suffering? Again, a
banal and tangential definition. Besides, even comedy
admits extreme forms of pain, horror, and suffering.
The character "type" in the comedy of manners is usually punished, if only by his own ridiculous appearance,
for his moderate vice. And how is one to balance guilt
and punishment accurately? Do we always succeed in
neutralizing the terror of a comic person by our superior knowledge which is denied to him? In other words,
is it really so easy to distinguish the ultimately harmless
or imaginary suffering and terror of comedy from the
real pain and terror of tragedy?

Even if it were, another difficult and much more crucial problem remains. Let us suppose that the pain and
suffering present in a given comedy or comical moment would *lose its harmlessness*, would cease to be neu-
tralized by the superior knowledge of the viewer. Does
this imply that its comical quality would get lost along
with the loss of the harmlessness of suffering? And does
it imply that what remains after this change is tragedy

pure and simple? There is something to be said for this view. All of us will have experienced the involuntary freezing of a smile when stark reality suddenly breaks through the veneer of comic harmlessness. And yet, this is not always and not necessarily a matter of either-or. For example, if one abruptly finds out one has been moving around in circles, be it metaphorically, in some significant activity or endeavor, or literally, this is, of course, the discovery of something ridiculous. But "if a wanderer who is about to die of thirst in a desert sets out in the morning in search of water and discovers in the evening that he has moved in a circle and has returned to his point of departure," we would certainly agree that there is something acutely bitter and even tragic, if we may use the term in a general fashion, about this circularity. Would it, however, for the same reason be "by no means comical"? [15] Certainly not. The familiar either-or pattern of thought fails in this case in the presence of the immediacy and certainty of the experience of the spectator (or even of the victim of the delusion). This experience is one of the identity and simultaneity of the "tragic" and the ludicrous in this moment of truth. And progressive "intellectual" analysis will by no means destroy the one or the other, the tragic or the comic, but will, on the contrary, realize in an infinitely deepened rational awareness, that both are, in fact, interdependent. The impression of tragic futility is surely not obliterated by the distinctly comic form and appearance that it takes. And, conversely, the aesthetic appreciation of the comic constellation, of the circular movement, is in no way weakened by the shrill tragic overtone that suddenly pierces our ears. More than that, full intellectual realization of the quality of such a scene or moment will make us aware that the tragic and the comic are here not only simultaneous and identical, but also that they heighten each other. That is: on the one hand, the tragic implication adds poignancy to the comic in giving it more depth or more obstacles to be "overcome" by laughter, making the comic incongruity all the more appreciable for its increased crassness. On the other hand, the undeniably comic constellation gives acumen to the bitterness of tragedy. And both kinds of interaction happen at once, depend on each other, and progressively and mutually increase each other. As G. Wilson Knight remarks in one of his essays on *King Lear*: "The comic and the tragic rest both on the idea of incompatibilities, and are also, themselves, mutually exclusive: therefore to mingle them is to add to the meaning of each; the result is but a new sublime incongruity." [16]

This is what happens in modern tragicomedy. In it the reciprocity of the interaction of the tragic and the comic is essential. In *comedy* the moments of "tragic" suffering or terror are merely designed to heighten our appreciation of the comic as the spectator realizes that suffering and terror have no actual basis in the reality of the situation. In *tragedy* a touch of judiciously placed comedy or irony is apt to enhance the tragic awareness, "on this condition," as Sarcey puts it, "that the disturbing element shall not interfere with the first impression, which should remain single, and that it shall even heighten that impression, by a slight effect of contrast." [17] E. T. A. Hoffmann even thought that "the most intense quality of tragedy had to be brought about by a special kind of jest." [18] The porter scene in *Macbeth* or the jests of the fool in *King Lear* may come to mind. This, of course, has little to do with so-called comic relief which, in medieval drama or in Shakespeare's histories for instance, merely serves to decrease the tension of our tragic involvement by temporarily diverting our attention to something entirely different. There is no chance with this kind of succession of the tragic and the comic for the synthetic view, for the very principle of the psychology of comic relief is that the comic scenes are experienced alternately with the tragic ones. This is indicated neatly in a German medieval passion play where a *praecursor* warns the audience against transposing the merriment of the comic interludes to the serious action[19] as well as in the Humanist Macropedius' prologue to his *Asotus* which admonishes the audience not to allow itself to be distracted from the sublime significance of the Biblical theme by the interspersed jocularity.

Only when both directions in the heightening of effect are integrated can we speak of the complex and yet simple phenomenon of the tragicomic. In it the comic and the tragic are identical and mutual conditions of each other. Edward Albee's *Who's Afraid of Virginia Woolf?*, at least throughout the greater part of the first two acts, is a particularly gripping example of this uncannily subtle, though painful integration at which we laugh with one eye and weep with the other. This play, like Dürrenmatt's *The Visit*, Ionesco's *The Chairs*, Harold Pinter's *The Caretaker* and so many others that have recently won international acclaim, proves that "the many psychologists" who "point out antipathy between strong emotions such as despair, anger, and hate and the perception of humor" (in the vague sense of anything ludicrous) must indeed be infrequent theatergoers to think that "a person evidently cannot experience both of these types of emotions at the same time" and that "any appreciation of humor on the part of a person lessens the degree of despair, anger, or hate which that person feels." [20] On the contrary, it may well be that the tragic is more tragic and the comic is more comic in the tragicomic fusion.

Let us turn now to some passages in well-known dramas where the phenomenon of the tragicomic, so far deduced theoretically, meets the eye. These plays are not tragicomedies in their entirety, but they have moments where the tragicomic is undeniably present. Does not one such moment occur in *King Lear* (III, vi, 45-46) when Lear institutes a mock trial of his daughters: "Arraign her first; 'tis Goneril. I here take my oath before this honorable assembly, she kicked the poor King her father." The first impression is probably a ludicrous one—a fool on the verge of insanity playing a childish game, totally incongruent with the dignity of the father and the king. Yet, at the same time, what a tragic disintegration, what a noble mind is here overthrown. There are similar moments of mixed feelings in Molière's *Tartuffe* when we are not sure whether to laugh or to cry at Orgon's deception by the protagonist. There is another at the end of Ibsen's *Hedda Gabler* as Tesman, Hedda's husband, not only innocently suggests that Hedda and Brack spend more time together, but says this precisely at the moment when it has become clear that this would be Hedda's undoing. A particularly good example is at the end of *Desire under the Elms* (Act III, Scene 1). The glimpse we obtain there of Old Cabot at the riotous party celebrating the birth of "his" son who is actually, and unbeknownst to him, the son of his young wife, Abbie, and his son Eben, is clearly tragicomic: overly game and bouncy, dancing in a delirium of fatherly bliss, cutting "incredibly grotesque capers," he is the butt of the stealthy jokes of the gossips who know who the real father is; and yet what a moving and gripping picture of the futility of Old Cabot's foolish but to him all-important endeavor to maintain a foothold in the world that he knows has been slipping all along. Or take another play by O'Neill, *A Moon for the Misbegotten*. At the end of the fourth act the lovers, Josie and Tyrone, find each other at last and realize their love for each other. But it is just then, in these moments of intimacy and trusting love, that it dawns upon Josie that Tyrone is irrevocably on the steep downhill path to ruin and that their wish will never be fulfilled. It is dawn. She sits in the farmyard in the moonlight, Tyrone's head in her lap; Tyrone is numb after one of his alcoholic excesses —a powerful image of total despair. At this point Josie *"forces a defensive, self-derisive smile:* 'God forgive me, it's a fine end to all my scheming, to sit here with the dead hugged to my breast, and the silly mug of the moon grinning down enjoying the joke.' " Karl Moor in Schiller's *Robbers* (Act III, Scene 2) voices a much more comprehensive tragicomic impression, in fact all but a *Weltanschauung*, when he says:

Brother, I have looked on men, their insect cares and their giant projects, their god-like plans and mouse-like occupations, their intensely eager race after happiness—one trusting to the fleetness of his horse, another to the nose of his ass, a third to his own legs; this checkered lottery of life, in which so many stake their innocence and their heaven to snatch a prize, and, blanks are all they draw—for they find, too late, that there was no prize in the wheel. It is a drama, brother, enough to bring tears into your eyes, while it shakes your sides with laughter.[21]

Friedrich Hebbel, the German dramatist and author of a play subtitled "Tragicomedy" (*Ein Trauerspiel in Sizilien, A Tragedy in Sicily*, 1851) described the experience of the tragicomic with particular forcefulness in the preface to that play: "One is about to freeze with horror, yet the muscles of risibility twitch at the same time. One would like to rid oneself of the entire uncanny impression by a laugh, yet a shiver overcomes us before we succeed in doing so." This describes roughly what since the eighteenth century has been called tragicomic (although it must be admitted that Hebbel's formulation smacks a little of the grotesque as well, which we shall have to distinguish from the tragicomic presently). At any rate, a historian of modern tragicomedy would do well to use this complex phenomenon of the tragicomic as the starting point and basis as well as the criterion for any discussion of the genre, for the *historical* concepts of the genre, which were analyzed in the first chapter, are no longer useful and meaningful categories for an understanding of modern tragicomedy.

While it may be relatively easy to demonstrate theoretically and practically the possibility of that synthetically tragicomic vision which identifies the opposites, it

is hard to speculate about its psychological causes. It
may be, as is frequently assumed, though not necessarily
in the wake of Freud, a conscious or unconscious defensive reaction. "The comic alone is able to give us the
strength to bear the tragedy of existence," Ionesco has
remarked. Nietzsche presumably meant the same in his
statement that "the most acutely suffering animal on
earth invented—laughter"; and Pirandello was report-
edly impressed by Macchiavelli's remark that he was in
the habit of laughing "to provide an outlet for my painful tears." [22] There is some evidence that audiences have
in fact reacted in this fashion to the performance of
tragedies. Still, one wonders if this is the whole truth
about the fascination of so many modern writers with
the tragicomic vision, for it should have become clear
from our discussion so far that the ingredient of the
comic by no means alleviates the pain of tragic awareness; on the contrary, it makes it more acute. The presence of the comic element, therefore, need not always
be interpreted as a symptom of escape or recourse to the
healing power of detachment. Rather than that, it may be
the result of a most serious urge to face unflinchingly
every bitter nuance of what is felt to be the tragedy of
existence. As such, the tragicomic vision as we have so
far developed it is a phenomenon not of escape, but of
courage, though some will always insist on their right to
call it decadence.

The Problem of Relativity

Having described the nature of the integration of the
comic and the tragic in the tragicomic synthesis, as precisely as is possible in such aesthetic disquisitions, our
argument is probably still open to one fundamental objection, namely that we have so far been using the terms
"the comic" and "the tragic" in a vague way which can,
at best, be justified, though dubiously, by common
usage. The objection is a natural one at this point. And

yet, the indefinite nature of our tentative definition, whatever its faults may be, is paradoxically one of its virtues, for it is only when one refuses to define a phenomenon dogmatically and narrowly at the outset of an investigation such as this that one has a chance of perceiving the wealth of the individual variations that it can have within literature itself. Each author is likely to have a view of the comic and the tragic which differs slightly from that of another author's. Obviously, if one does not make allowances for such differences, that is, if one uses an inflexible yardstick for the assessment of one and all plays under discussion, one would blind oneself to a good many tragicomedies which, though not like the supposedly more "standard" or more typical plays of this kind, are nonetheless of interest. Terminological exactitude at the beginning of a genre study invariably boomerangs in the sense that it results in an unjustifiable distortion of the total picture.

Still, there is one major danger inherent in such loose use of terms essential to our problem. We might call it perspectivism. Not only do critics and, apparently, the general audience, too, quarrel about the precise location of the borderline between the comic and the tragic, but also about the identity of both. Theatergoers or not, we are all familiar with this confusion: in the theater people laugh in the "wrong places," adults will smile about the sorrows of children, children will laugh about the misfortunes of adults. Such types of confusion can, of course, be resolved easily by determining which reaction could reasonably be expected to be adequate. But there are much more intriguing and elusive cases. Temporal distance may diametrically change our reaction to a given work of art. Change in taste plays some very curious tricks on some works of art, often making the history of the appraisal of a given work or body of comparable works a story of misunderstandings, some productive, some not. Nor is it always the inherent richness of content and experience or the ambivalence of intention in a work of art that causes such radical divergence in appreciation. Thus, some bona fide tragedies like Ibsen's *The Master Builder*, Victor Hugo's *Hernani*, Pietro Metastasio's *Forsaken Dido*, Marlowe's *Tamburlaine*, Lessing's *Miss Sara Sampson*, naturalistic tragedies such as Sudermann's and A. W. Pinero's as well as expressionistic dramas of frustration nowadays tend to arouse smiles and laughter in an average audience or reader. One critic even managed to see a comedy in Gerhart Hauptmann's *Weavers*—which, no doubt, presupposes a more modern and progressive view of the methods of social reform than most people have. T. S. Eliot quite seriously suggested that if one tried to read Marlowe's tragedy *The Jew of Malta* as a farce it might be appreciated more by modern audiences.[23]

On the other hand, increased historical distance might teach us to see the tragic in what was at the time meant to be comedy pure and simple. Molière's plays are a case in point. Modern scholarship is agreed that the author intended his dramas to be comic and nothing but comic. "Molière never wrote, nor wished to write, anything but comedies which were comedies, from beginning to end," F. Sarcey stated as early as 1876. But ever since Rousseau's *Lettre à d'Alembert sur les spectacles* (1758), at least *Le Misanthrope* has been considered to be a play in the tragicomic mode, or even tragicomedy par excellence. At least one other of Molière's comedies, *Tartuffe*, has, again since the eighteenth century been viewed similarly (Moses Mendelssohn in his *Rhapsody on the Sensations*, 1761) while some modern critics would be inclined to add *Georges Dandin* and perhaps still others. The Romantics re-evaluated Aristophanes in a comparable fashion, seeing in his seemingly light-hearted farces touches of metaphysical woe and catastrophe. Enlightenment critics had somewhat similar problems with Terence, and so on. Conversely, it may be generations before the audience is ready to realize the comic intentions of an author as, for example, in the case

of Gogol's *Inspector-General* (1836) which depressed
the contemporaries for whom the satire was too close
to home to be enjoyed as light-heartedly as it is by
modern audiences. Particularly telling is Prince V. F.
Odoyevsky's letter to a friend after reading A. N. Ostrovsky's drama *It's a Family Affair—We'll Settle It Ourselves:* "Have you read," he writes,

> Ostrovsky's comedy, or rather tragedy, *It's a Family Af-
> fair—We'll Settle It Ourselves*, the real title of which is *The
> Bankrupt?* It is time to expose spiritually the class of people
> whose spirit is most corrupt. If this is not a momentary flash,
> not a mushroom, saturated with rot of every kind, springing
> of its own accord out of the earth, he is a man of enormous
> talent. In Russia there are in my judgment three tragedies:
> *The Minor, Woe from Wit*, and *The Inspector-General*. I
> am betting on *The Bankrupt* as number four.

A modern audience or reader would hardly agree that
Gogol's play is a tragedy. The temporal distance does,
however, not need to be quite so great. For changes of
taste that take place within a more limited time-span,
translations can sometimes be reliable and interesting in-
dicators. Thus, Matthew Gregory Lewis' tragedy *The
Castle Spectre* (1797) was translated into German at a
time when such gothic horror-mongering was no longer
taken seriously as a respectable form of theatrical entertainment. The title of the German version reads *Die
lustige Tragödie oder die tragische Komödie von dem
Burggespenst Eveline (The Merry Tragedy or Tragic
Comedy of the Castle Spectre Evelina)*.[24]

But changes in taste are by no means the only reason
for a confusion of the tragic and the comic. Cultural
differences may be equally responsible. This is too obvious to require further demonstration. Alan R. Thompson has reminded us, for instance, that "a Chinese play
. . . may move orientals to tears and yet strike Ameri-
cans as merely odd or funny." Nor need the cultural
difference be quite so marked. Some critics find Ibsen's
A Doll's House funny, others tragic.[25]

This disturbing relativity of the comic and the tragic is probably most disconcerting when there is a discrepancy between the author's intention and the audience's reaction. Ionesco professes that he was shocked to learn that his audiences mistook *Les Chaises* (*The Chairs*) for comedy, for he was convinced that he had written a tragedy.[26] With Chekhov it was just the other way round: He took great pains in his letters to point out that *The Cherry Orchard* was meant to be funny, not sad as the contemporary viewers believed.

Another source of confusion is to be found, of course, in those variations of the style of performance, the possibility of which most authors try to eliminate in various ways, to be sure, but without any guarantee of success. It is certainly doubtful that *every* tragedy can be performed as comedy, but there are some that lend themselves to such distortion more easily than others. "Richard III was played for comedy by Irving, but for pathos by Olivier," J. L. Styan has noted, and Brecht remarked to Eric Bentley on a performance of his *Caucasian Chalk Circle* that Ernst Busch had missed the "whole tragic side of the role" of Azdak, the judge, and had seen only the comic side. Ionesco was troubled by the knowledge that his *Rhinocéros*, with its only thinly disguised topical appeal ("Nazification of a country") had been transformed into very different kinds of plays by the style of performance: "Stroux, the director in Düsseldorf, and his leading actor, Karl Maria Schley, turned it into a stark tragedy with no concessions, barely relieved by its cold irony; the Poles made it a weighty play. But Mr. Antoni, acting on the advice of Heaven-knows-who, and certainly not the author, has made it into something funny and anti-conformist." On the other hand, Ionesco thought nothing of pointing out, with more generosity than critical acumen, in the same year and in the same journal, that "both interpretations [that is: "tragedy" and "farce"] are valid, exemplary productions of this play." [27]

To add to this array of sorry facts, it may even be that this relativity of the comic and the tragic can, in some cases, also be a matter of the difference between reading and seeing a play. Jan Kott, the eminent Polish Shakespeare critic who has recently received a fair amount of attention in the West, claims that *Titus Andronicus* is ludicrous on account of its atrocities when one reads it, but deeply moving and gripping when seen on stage; from this he draws the conclusion that *Titus Andronicus*, an early play, is already Shakespearean theater, but not yet Shakespearean text.[28]

Enough of these ambivalences, the audience's and the drama's. These examples would seem to prove that the comic and the tragic are largely a matter of the educational, cultural, historical, or philosophical point of view of the theatergoer, who threatens the scholar bent on neat classifications with the infinite relativity of terms. We could shrug our shoulders and jump to the conclusion that Rosso di San Secondo found the incontrovertible answer to the problem when he subtitled one of his later plays "Farce or tragedy, depending on the whim of the audience." [29]

Naturally, no author or critic worth his salt would want to leave such decisions to the fickle audience. The trouble is, however, that the relativity we have so far discussed is not merely the product of the comparatively uncritical thinking and untrained responses of the average theatergoer. Even critics disagree, for as Jerome Stolnitz has pointed out, one critic's meat may be another's poison: what one aesthetic thinker considers the perfect definition of tragedy could serve another critic as perfectly adequate for the theory of comedy. Thus, young Goethe in his Shakespeare speech of 1771 defined the tragic as the clash between the great individual and the "inevitable course of the whole." Stefan Schütze, the Romantic theoretician, thought that this would be the ideal formula for comedy. Vice versa, Justus Möser's concept of the comic, that is, greatness without strength, is viewed as a "profoundly sad" if not tragic condition by a modern writer on the theory of tragedy. G. Wilson Knight has taught us to see in *King Lear* a piece of grim metaphysical fun which it probably takes a god to enjoy. Likewise, it would help to be a god, or, barring that, a professor of dialectical philosophy, to appreciate the thesis of the American philosopher J. Loewenberg who believes that not any one tragedy, such as *King Lear*, is profoundly comical but *all* tragedy per se.[30]

A glance at dramatic theory is, then, small comfort. So is a glance at literary criticism. There are, for instance, certain well-known literary characters whose names have almost become household words in the educated world who seem to defy any scholarly attempt to classify them as either comic or tragic to everybody's satisfaction: Don Quixote, Shylock, Mendoza (in John Marston's *Malcontent*), Shakespeare's Timon, Molière's Alceste (*Le Misanthrope*), and Orgon (*Tartuffe*).

Overcoming Relativity: The Demarcation and Structure of Tragicomedy

Like naive audiences, then, trained criticism and literary theory would not seem to offer a way out of our dilemma; rather than that, they only deepen it and make it all the more disconcerting that the tragic and the comic can so effortlessly lose their identities. As a result —and here we return to our main question—*tragicomedy* would seem to be a bird more unlikely than the dodo ever was. But this only seems so. Unless one wants to indulge in the philosophical pleasures of speculating *about* literature rather than turning an attentive ear to the language of literature itself, there are two ways of extracting oneself from the dilemma of relativity. First, one could make an effort to distinguish the phenomenon of the tragicomic from related phenomena such as the grotesque and the melodramatic. Secondly, one could try to grasp certain structural devices, recurrent throughout the history of modern tragicomedy, by which the phenomenon of the tragicomic is produced in the receptive imagination of the audience. This double endeavor necessitates a somewhat academically abstract *étude*, but its advantage is that our concept of the tragicomic is further clarified in the process.

Turning to the problem of demarcation first, we notice that the phenomenon of the tragicomic has a goodly number of relatives which, almost without exception, have at one time or another been identified with it. Several, in fact most, of these identifications are luckily rather uncalled for and can, therefore, be dealt with summarily. For example, it should require only a smattering of critical awareness to distinguish parody and travesty from tragicomedy although both are sometimes confused with it, as in Karl Mahlke's *Moderne Tragikomödien* (1882). Nor should it be difficult to distinguish between the curiously mixed sensation of the "joy of grief," so dear to the "sentimental" age, and the experience of the tragicomic, if only for the reason that there is no awareness of the comic in the "joy of grief" unless one mistakes the egocentrically emotional, self-pitying half-smile on a tear-stained face for it, which would be arbitrary indeed.

The melodramatic mode, on the other hand, does combine the "comic" with the "tragic," but the result is not tragicomic for two reasons. First, the comic is, more often than not, of the claptrap, stagy variety, wildly exaggerated and fantastically improbable, while the "tragic" (if we may call it that for a moment) is a matter of horror, bloody sensationalism, and a lachrymosity which will strike the average viewer as just barely missing involuntary ludicrousness. That is, in melodrama, the component phenomena are neither truly comic nor truly tragic. Stretching the meaning of these two terms to include the sensations produced by melodrama would be generous to a fault. Secondly, the elements of melodrama, such as they are, do not fuse in the same fashion as the comic and the tragic blend in the tragicomic but are, rather, juxtaposed, cleverly at times, but still without fusion or integration.

With satire, so frequently identified with tragicomedy, the case is different. There we find a combination of high and often bitter seriousness and incisive ludicrousness, and the combination, in this case, means a much closer union of the two than it does in melodrama. What drives the satirist to caricature an objectionable reality is nothing but the pain of being aware that this particular segment of reality (usually of social reality) is wrong, perverse, evil, or lacking in essential substance, and this pain is obvious in the distorted image of the world he presents. This presupposes that the satirist in his contempt of what *is* knows, by contrast, what and how reality *should be*. This, in turn, means that his criticism (for that is what satire basically purports to be) is leveled at reality from an unshakably firm standpoint, from a sure knowledge of norm and ideal. Thus, the satirist shares, on the one hand, an essential aspect of his art with the comic writer, though in his works the comic has a painfully bitter overtone which makes satire distinct from all other forms of comic writing. On the other hand, the satirist parts company with the tragic and the tragicomic writer because neither proceeds from such a secure starting point in his creative examination of reality. They, on the contrary, feel that it is precisely the questionability of such supposedly unshakable and knowable points of human orientation that drives them to their apprehension of reality in their artistic production. The tragicomic writer, even more so than the tragic writer, tends to leave his audience not only in a state of indecision as to whether to laugh or to weep, but also in a more profound and disturbing disorientation to the human condition. This, however, is not the reaction we have when viewing a satiric play, a satiric comedy such as Gogol's *Inspector-General* or Molière's

Les Précieuses Ridicules or Shaw's comedies. The author's own designation for his work may be misleading in this respect. Thus, Zuckmayer's *Hauptmann von Köpenick* (*The Colonel of Coepenick*), though the author himself designated it as "tragicomedy" in his English autobiography, *Second Wind*,[31] is a satire, arousing, as it does, the somewhat forced laughter of scorn and derision. Friedrich Hebbel, too, called his basically satiric play *Ein Trauerspiel in Sizilien* (*A Tragedy in Sicily*) a tragicomedy. But it was particularly George Bernard Shaw, satirist par excellence, who identified tragicomedy and satire. In the preface to *Major Barbara* (1905), in the section entitled "First Aid to Critics," he claimed: "I deal in the tragicomic irony of the conflict between real life and the Romantic imagination," that is: between what people are and what they imagine or want to be. This is clarified a bit further at the end of the preface to volume two of *Plays: Pleasant and Unpleasant* (1898) where he says: "To me the tragedy and comedy of life lie in the consequences, sometimes terrible, sometimes ludicrous, of our persistent attempts to found our institutions on the ideals suggested to our imaginations by our half-satisfied passions, instead of a genuinely scientific natural history." This would imply that tragicomedy is only a historical social phenomenon of limited duration, to be overcome by more progressive social ideals. And Shaw says as much in his Tolstoy essay of 1921. Ibsen, he claims there,

was the dramatic poet who firmly established tragi-comedy as a much deeper and grimmer entertainment than tragedy. His heroes dying without hope or honor, his dead, forgotten, superseded men walking and talking with the ghosts of the past, are all heroes of comedy: their existence and their downfall are not soul-purifying convulsions of pity and horror, but reproaches, challenges, criticisms addressed to society and to the spectator as a voting constituent of society. They are miserable and yet not hopeless; for they are mostly criticisms of false intellectual positions which, being intellectual, are remediable by better thinking.[32]

Like the satirist, the humorist, too, has his feet firmly planted on a ground that gives meaning to his life and his endeavors and makes, in fact, his humor possible. This statement implies, of course, that we do not use the word humor in the vague and all-inclusive sense that makes it tantamount to the perception and expression of anything laughable, but in the more specific sense that has evolved since the critical discussions of nineteenth-century aestheticians and has been formulated most cogently by the Danish philosopher Harald Høffding in his book *Den Store Humor* (*The Grand Humor*). Accordingly, the vision of the humorist encompasses the great and the small things in the world, pleasures and sufferings, worth and worthlessness, becoming and perishing, the tragic and the comic—but all this is seen from the firm standpoint of knowing tolerance or, to use a different image, it is seen within the framework of a world that is intact. The humorist sees himself securely settled within a cosmic horizon that provides the comfort of reassurance and may even enable him to believe in an all-encompassing divine principle. The mingling of clowns and kings in medieval drama has thus been explained as humor on the part of the authors of such plays. However, the tragicomedian, as distinguished from the humorist, lacks precisely this ultimate reassurance. When he views the comic as tragic and the tragic as comic, he is face to face with the questionability of the smaller or greater scheme of things and denies himself the firm footing that more fortunate writers have. Or rather: if there is one thing he is sure of, it is that this firm footing can only be gained temporarily and precariously, for it is constantly threatened. Thus, the tragicomedian, more often than not, is exposed to the challenge of ultimate and total meaninglessness, without, however, necessarily falling prey to it. This cannot be said about the humorist. For him the "tragic" invariably loses the bitter and despairing quality which it tends to have for the tragicomedian. In fact, for the humorist the tragic is in danger of being reduced to the merely serious and sad. This variety of the tragic he either juxtaposes with the comic, or he fuses the two in a blend that might be characterized by half-smiling melancholy or the mood of understanding wisdom. The tone of ultimate reassurance is essential to both.

If this reassurance is lost, if one has the sensation of losing one's grip of reality and one's foothold in life, one is likely to be confronted with the grotesque or the absurd. Essential to both is disorientation. In fact, they can be viewed as the two sides of one and the same coin: the grotesque is, by and large, the outward appearance of the absurd, that is to say: the disorienting perception of the absurdity of the world expresses itself in the modern "theater of the absurd" by means of a distortion of reality which is grotesque. Or to put it still differently, the grotesque is largely an aesthetic category, the absurd a philosophical one, and both are suited to each other like "form" and "content." What the grotesque-absurd has in common with the tragicomic is its disorientation. Yet this is no reason for identifying the two as is so frequently done, for the quality of disorientation is significantly different. The grotesque (we use this term in preference to the clumsy "grotesque-absurd") implies ludicrous horror or horrifying ludicrousness. Its fantastic distortions of reality make us apprehend, in a cold shudder, something abysmally uncanny and demonic, an awareness which generates the feelings of estrangement, stupefying bafflement, strained laughter and gruesome fright and anguish all at the same time. There is, therefore, something of the comic, to be sure, but only a very remote touch of the tragic in this fusion of emotions and sensations that modern critics call grotesque. The best label for this fusion would be uncanniness: uncanniness from whose horror laughter *hopes* to provide momentary relief but rather succeeds in making the horror all the more obvious through this very gesture of escape. The grotesque is the vision of an absurdity, usually of cosmic dimension, which defies all intellectual efforts to clarify and elucidate its possible meaning in terms of human understanding. One of the charms of the tragicomic, on the other hand, is the possibility to think through, almost ad infinitum, the complicated mechanism by which the comic and the tragic are intertwined and indeed identified. Tragicomedy remains within the confines of logic and what is generally accepted as the common characteristics of reality. It refuses to distort the world in such a way that we find it hard to recognize it as ours. The grotesque play, the theater of the absurd, on the contrary, would be deficient in an essential ingredient if it did not do precisely this. Weird and fantastic things happen in grotesque plays that would be unthinkable in the more traditional concept of reality that tragicomedy is bound by. Ionesco has listed some, using his own plays as illustrations:

countless mushrooms sprout in the flat of Amédée and Madeleine; a dead body suffering from geometric progression grows there too and turns the tenants out; in *Victims of Duty*, when coffee is to be served to three of the characters, there is a mounting pile of hundreds of cups [proliferating themselves automatically]; the furniture in *The New Tenant* first blocks up every staircase in the building, then clutters the stage and finally entombs the character who came to take a room in the house [it should be added that the stream of furniture moves in automatically, without the aid of man or machine]; in *The Chairs* the stage is filled with dozens of chairs for invisible guests; and in *Jack* several noses appear on the face of a young girl.[33]

One could easily add to these grotesqueries of modern theater: legless people live in garbage cans (Beckett's *Endgame*); an ugly woman is shot and thereby transformed into a beautiful princess (Ionesco's *The Picture*); a rare disease, rhinoceritis, turns people into rhinoceroses (Ionesco's *Rhinocéros*); in a grotesque brothel it is not beyond the girls to discard, along with their clothes, their cheeks, eyes, and other parts of the body until only the skeleton remains (Jean Tardieu's *La Serrure* [*The Lock*]); the dead arise (Tardieu's *Qui est là?* [*Who Is There?*]); people are transformed into works of art and packed in boxes to be shipped (Wolfgang Hildesheimer's *Landschaft mit Figuren* [*Landscape with Figures*]); or they can have coins for eyes, the mouthpiece of a telephone for a mouth, and an antenna-equipped radio for a forehead (Ivan Goll's *Methusalem*). The time in a grotesque play may be summer and winter simultaneously, as in Jarry's *Ubu Roi* (*King Ubu*), and the place a northern and a southern landscape to be seen from the same room, as in Dürrenmatt's *Die Ehe des Herrn Mississippi* (*The Marriage of Mr. Mississippi*).

Tragicomedy spares us such unsettling experiences. They are, however, part and parcel of the nightmarish world of the grotesque and the absurd. The writer of grotesque plays, as Martin Esslin contends in the concluding chapter of his *Theater of the Absurd*, is shocked and troubled by the loss of "ultimate certainties" and meaningful purposes in the world. So is the writer of tragicomedies. The difference is that the writer of grotesque plays attempts to shock his audience into an awareness of this human condition by the extreme distortion of reality that has been described; the author of tragicomedies is more conventionally "realistic" in his use of means to a similar end. He refuses to dispense with logic and the common mien of reality, with verisimilitude. Thus, while the grotesque theater represents a world that has gone so mad that it is impossible to understand its madness, tragicomedy represents a world that is not so much nonsensical, as it is out-of-joint, with the parts still intact. As such, it is viewed by the author and, hopefully, the audience, not with the conscious abandon of reason, but with a reason that is sorely concerned and afflicted and grows constantly more so as it discovers the comical nature of the tragedy it endeavors to grasp.

These differentiations may sharpen our eyes for the perception of the tragicomic and clarify our unreflected sensitivity to this aesthetic phenomenon as well as to its manner of expression in literature. But they do not go all the way towards eliminating the problem of the relativity of the comic and the tragic (and the resulting arbitrariness of interpretation) which led us to them in the first place. The genuine tragicomic could be identified more reliably than on the basis of the comparative criterion discussed so far if one had some knowledge of the specific ways and means by which the tragicomic vision of the author is realized in drama so that the audience reacts with the corresponding sensation.

This is all the more important because the phenomenon of the tragicomic can obviously appear in narrative forms of literature as well as in drama. In fact, José Ortega y Gasset expressed the view that the tragicomic mode was the earmark of any and all narrative fiction.[34] This may or may not be the case. Still, an effort should be made to distinguish the manner of organization and articulation of subject matter by which the sensation of the tragicomic is brought about in narrative and dramatic writing, respectively. In so doing, one should be able to arrive at certain structural criteria which would help to verify any preliminary impression (when reading a play) that one is or is not dealing with tragicomedy. The validity of such structural criteria would, of course, have to be derived from familiarity with a wide selection of tragicomedies. Needless to add, the establishment of structural criteria for a genre is of particular significance for the study of a *dramatic* genre because there are no easily identifiable criteria (of the externally formal variety) to guide us in our quest for a specific kind of drama. While a given poem can readily be identified as a sonnet, for example, by the most casual glance at its stanzaic pattern and rhyme scheme, the structural criteria of tragicomedy are not that apparent.

In narrative fiction, then, the realization of the tragicomic is primarily a matter of the attitude and perspective of the narrator. Whether he is specifically introduced as a more or less distinct fictitious personality or merely expressed in the particular way in which the prose style addresses itself to the reader, the narrator is invariably an essential element of any narrative (with the possible, though by no means certain, exception of some stream-of-consciousness novels and the present-day *nouveau roman* of Alain Robbe-Grillet, Natalie Sarraute, and others). And it is easy to see that such a narrator (who is, of course, not identical with the author, but a fictitious *persona*) will have no difficulty in predisposing the reader towards a tragicomic vision of the narrated subject matter, if the author so desires. This is merely a matter of the interpretative comment of the narrator which is well-nigh inevitable in fiction anyway.

The dramatist, it is true, could use a similar technique by introducing a *raisonneur* or commentator (as in Arthur Miller's *View from the Bridge* or John Osborne's *Entertainer* and most plays of the Brechtian "epic" theater). Such a *raisonneur* could suggest the tragicomic reaction to the audience. Or the dramatist could use two such *raisonneurs*, as Cocteau did in *Bacchus* and Pirandello in *Six Characters in Search of an Author*, one making the audience aware of the comic potentialities of the material, the other pointing out its tragic qualities. Still, this remains in effect a device which is more germane to narrative fiction, and the dramatist is by no means limited to it. In fact, any survey would show that dramatists rarely use it, and if they do, it is, more often than not, in a purely auxiliary function.

If the dramatist deprives himself of the benefit of a *raisonneur* in his attempt to write a tragicomedy, he has no choice but to create the cosmos of his drama in such a way that the tragicomic vision is suggested to the viewer, with forcefulness and inevitability, by the peculiar shape and organization of this cosmos itself. That is, the writer of tragicomedy objectifies and concretizes his own tragicomic vision by articulating his subject matter according to certain structural patterns which then also generate a corresponding receptive vision in the audience. These structural patterns are precisely the ones which constitute the shape (*morphé, Gestalt*) of the play. The history of modern tragicomedy shows that there are indeed such morphological constants in which the *double entendre*, the ambiguity specific to the genre, is crystallized. What, then, are these structural patterns that suggest the tragicomic vision to the audience?

A brief descriptive survey must suffice in this context. Nothing short of a detailed and lengthy analysis of a large number of tragicomedies could demonstrate how these structural patterns actually function.

The most easily identifiable of these patterns to emerge from any full-scale study of tragicomedy is the one that contrasts a character fit for tragedy with a world that distinctly belongs to the realm of comedy. Molière's *Misanthrope*, now almost universally held to be a tragicomic play rather than a farce, is a case in point. Alceste, with his insistent earnestness bent on profound and meaningful human relations, is a character right out of tragedy and a misfit in a social world where the flippancy and frivolity of comedy reign supreme. The particular incongruence of a potentially tragic person and his comic surroundings which makes his aspirations appear comic has been exploited by other writers of tragicomedies: Shakespeare in *Troilus and Cressida*, Heinrich von Kleist in *Amphitryon*, Reinhold Lenz in *Tantalus*, John Davidson in his "tragic farce" *Smith*, Jean Anouilh in *Colombe*, and Friedrich Dürrenmatt in *Der Besuch der alten Dame* (*The Visit*). It has even been argued that this is the only type of tragicomedy possible.[35] But this is certainly not so as any familiarity with the subject will show. For instance, the converse incongruence is equally thinkable: an essentially comic person (though capable of the tragic by virtue of his human worth and

depth) finds himself in the world of tragedy and is overcome by it. Chekhov's *Cherry Orchard,* one of the most
outstanding tragicomedies of the modern era, comes to
mind, as well as some German plays such as J.M.R.
Lenz's *Die Soldaten* (*The Soldiers*) and *Der Hofmeister*
(*The Private Tutor*), Georg Büchner's *Woyzeck,*
Franz Werfel's *Jacobowski und der Oberst* (*Jacobowski and the Colonel*), even Wedekind's *Frühlingser-
wachen* (*Spring's Awakening*), and most recently, Karl
Wittlinger's *Kennen Sie die Milchstrasse?* (*Do You
Know the Milky Way?*) which the author, in his prefa-
tory account of the genesis of the play, calls tragicomedy. The best example in French literature is no
doubt Cocteau's *Bacchus.* In English literature, O'Casey's *The Plough and the Stars* comes very close to this
variety of tragicomedy. In Scandinavian drama Odd
Eidem's *Spillet om Bly-Petter* (*Play on Lead-Peter*) suggests itself; and an interesting variation is presented in
Knut Hamsun's *Livet Ivold* (*In the Grip of Life*) whose
symbolic *leitmotif* is "running aground with full sails."
This refers to the hectic and forced hilarity of a corrupt
society against the background of its imminent disastrous end: a dance on the volcano.

Another easily identifiable pattern combines two parallel plots of equal weight, one tragic, one comic, which
are linked by a common theme and comparable motifs.
As a subordinate device this technique is perhaps best
known from Shakespeare's *Antony and Cleopatra,*
where the love of the protagonists is paralleled by the
love of the comical pair Alexas and Charmian, but, of
course, this parallel is only momentary and is not
enough to make the play a tragicomedy. Likewise, in
Marlowe's *Doctor Faustus,* Faust's pact with Mephisto-
pheles is paralleled in the manner of parody by Wag-
ner's pact with the clown, and there are some other such
partial tragic-comic parallels in this play. The best example, however, of a fully articulated tragic-comic parallelism of theme and motifs, one that is sustained

throughout the entire duration of the drama, is *The Changeling* (1653) by Thomas Middleton and William Rowley. Here, the plots are distinctly related in their basic theme and motifs, even down to such details as imagery. Moreover, there are explicit cross references and deliberate echos and reflections of the one plot on the other and vice versa, each commenting on the other. The overall result of this is, of necessity, that the tragic love involvements gain a shade of the comic, the comic ones a shade of the tragic; tragic disaster and ludicrous failure blend into a complex unity, into an atmosphere which makes this play an early tragicomedy of remarkable distinction.[36] This device, it will be understood, is not easy to realize successfully: if the cross references are too explicit, they may strike us as trite. If they are not explicit enough, the desired effect may be lost on the audience. Friedrich Maximilian Klinger tried his hand at it and failed (*Das leidende Weib* |*The Suffering Woman*] and *Sturm und Drang* [*Storm and Stress*]); Alfred Neumann called his *Frauenschuh* a tragicomedy because of this technique, but it is hardly a good play. Christian Dietrich Grabbe was relatively successful with this device in his philosophical play *Don Juan und Faust* which consistently confronts the two mythic figures of world literature as the comic lover and the tragic lover: one and the same posture is reflected, so to speak, by two distorting mirrors; in one we see Don Juan as a ludicrous figure, in the other Faust as a tragic one. Ruggiero Leoncavallo, finally, used the parallelism of theme and motif with a fair degree of success in his libretto *Bajazzo*. One may argue that this technique has its archetype in the convention in medieval mystery plays of parodying the main serious action by a comic sub-plot. It survived on the popular stage until, at least, the eighteenth century. A Viennese Faust play of that century "parodistically confronted the tragic hero, whose fate even in this version still has a deeply moving effect, step by step with a comical figure." [37]

A fourth, also somewhat crude type of tragicomedy has already been mentioned in the concluding section of the first chapter: a comic person bringing about tragic disaster for others. This, it will be remembered, was Hebbel's definition; it has frequently been repeated, but there are no really successful tragicomedies conforming to this pattern.

A much more subtle device, which, like all preceding ones, exploits the disproportion between the character and his surroundings, can be described as "deception." It is familiar in such tragicomedies as Molière's *Georges Dandin*, Ibsen's *The Wild Duck*, Ionesco's *The Chairs*, Lorca's *Doña Rosita*, Julius Bab's *Der Andere (The Other One)*, Stefan Zweig's *Das Lamm des Armen (The Poor Man's Lamb)*, Strindberg's *Fordringsägare (Creditors)*, Georg Kaiser's *König Hahnrei (King Cuckold)*, Hjalmar Bergman's *The Markurells of Wadkoeping*, and others. This technique depends for its effect on the integration of two worlds: on the one hand, the world of properly understood realities and, on the other, the imaginary world of the main figure which deviates from the former world. The protagonist lives in his world of illusion while the audience, sometimes along with some of the characters on stage, knows that what he believes to be real is, in fact, not. This discrepancy may be the result of self-deception or deceptive maneuvering by others, or of both, as is usually the case in tragicomedies on the cuckold theme. At any rate, this discrepancy of the real and the imaginary worlds, their conflict and, occasionally, their ultimate clash that destroys the illusion, can be seen as comic and tragic at the same time. Thus, Malvolio is a tragicomic figure, though *Twelfth Night* is not a tragicomic play throughout. The essential prerequisite for this tragicomic effect is, however, that the victim of the deception is not merely a comic "type," that is: a character devoid of that human depth and worth and substance that could make him potentially tragic. For example, the cuckold belongs in the sphere of farce; if he is duped we laugh at him, more or less satirically. Yet, if the cuckold is at the same time also a man of human worth and profundity of character as Amphitryon in Kleist's play (but unlike the Amphitryon in Molière's comedy), then, and only then, does he belong to the world of tragicomedy and we laugh at him with one eye weeping. That he could also belong to the sphere of tragedy is conceivable, in spite of the predominantly comical nature of the underlying constellation of the plot. But there seems to have been no attempt as yet by any dramatist to place him there.

The tragicomic discrepancy between man and world can also be articulated in quite a different fashion which has enjoyed almost equal popularity with writers of tragicomedies the world over. This device we might call "irony of the course of events." Unlike the ones discussed so far, it does not seem to depend so much on the interaction of the protagonist and his surroundings, but only seemingly, for though this device undeniably places more emphasis on the "events," on the particular nature and manner of the sequence of events, this is, obviously, always a course of events which affects one or more of the leading characters, in fact victimizes them. Goethe, in his famous Shakespeare speech of 1771 thought that tragedy was brought about in Shakespeare's plays by the clash of the individual and the "inevitable course of the whole." While this is less descriptive of Shakespeare's histories and tragedies than of Goethe's own, it is clear that tragedy could indeed be derived from such a "clash"—or comedy, for that matter, as Stefan Schütze thought in his book on the theory of the comic in 1817 (*Versuch einer Theorie des Komischen*). A particular way of devising this course of events could also result in tragicomedy as it did in Lascelles Abercrombie's *Phoenix*, Galsworthy's *Skin Game*, Eduard Stucken's *Die Gesellschaft des Abbé Châteauneuf* (*Abbé Châteauneuf's Soirée*), all designated as tragicomedies by their authors. Other plays, though not expressly declared tragicomedies, employ the same device: Ibsen's *Little Eyolf*, Strindberg's *There Are Crimes and Crimes*, J. M. Synge's *The Well of Saints*, Sean O'Casey's "tragicomedy" *The Silver Tassie*, Herwarth Walden's *Trieb* (*Desire*) and *Letzte Liebe* (*Last Love*), Ernst Toller's *Masse Mensch*, Schnitzler's *Der junge Medardus* (*Young Medardus*), and some of the early playlets of Hofmannsthal, like *Der weisse Fächer* (*The White Fan*) and *Die Hochzeit der Sobeide* (*The Wedding of Sobeide*). Cyril Tourneur's *Revenger's Tragedy* comes close to this type of tragicomedy but falls short of it if examined in detail. In this type of play, the course of events is contrived in such a way that it is invariably ironic; yet the *dramatis personae* trapped by this ironic course of events rise to the stature of tragic heroes under its impact. The philosophical implications suggested in such tragicomedies are hard to overlook and frequently are stated quite expressly: ultimately it is fate, or God, or Providence (albeit Baudelaire's "providence diabolique") that brings about this painfully, indeed tragically, ironic course of events. If the world of tragicomedies constructed on this pattern is dominated by any superior, metaphysical power at all, it is by that evil god who has exerted such a powerful fascination on generations of post-Enlightenment writers until the present day.

But perhaps the subtlest devices (though not so fraught with philosophical or theological content) of tragicomic integration are those that are based on the structure of the main character or characters of a play.*

---

* This is not contrary to our general observation that the conflict of man and his world is a constitutive element of all drama and tragicomedy, in particular. In the devices discussed below, this conflict is merely internalized. If a character is made up of conflicting traits, one of these invariably represents what the "world" expects of the particular *dramatis persona* or sees in him or makes him believe he "is," etc. A character consisting essentially of one dominant, exaggerated trait, on the other hand, is, by this very exaggeration, contrasted with the golden mean which his "world" is aware of—as well as the audience and, sometimes, the protagonist himself.

A common one exploits a conflict within a person, such
as the discrepancy between intention and fulfillment,
wish and being, a person's ideal concept of himself and
his reality, artist and human being, body and mind, being and mask, and so on. Victor Hugo, in his epoch-
making plea for tragicomedy, the preface to his drama
Cromwell (1827), which is at the same time the manifesto of French Romanticism against Classicism, conceives of this structural pattern when he talks about the
"drama, which with the same breath molds . . . tragedy and comedy." He considered this "the distinguishing characteristics of . . . the literature of the present
day." "Men of genius," he says, for example,

however great they be, have always within them a touch
of the beast which mocks at their intelligence. Therein they
are akin to mankind in general, for therein they are dramatic. "It is but a step from the sublime to the ridiculous,"
said Napoleon, when he was convinced that he was mere
man; and that outburst of a soul on fire illumines art and
history at once; that cry of anguish is the résumé of the
drama and of life.[38]

To be more specific: this device of internal character
dichotomy realizes its tragicomic effect by exploiting
the two sides of the *dramatis persona* in such a way that
they not only offset each other, but impart their aesthetic quality (comic and tragic, respectively) to each
other. Thus, a ludicrously disproportioned physiognomy may make an isolated noble mind all the more
tragic in its suffering while the contrast with the highly
valuable human substance will make the shortcomings of
the outward appearance all the more comical, as in Ed-
mond Rostand's *Cyrano de Bergerac*. Or, as in O'Neill's
A Touch of the Poet, the ludicrously unfitting role only
increases the tragedy of the man who had to resort to it
out of the very suffering that is at the root of his being
while the awareness of this psychological state behind
the mask makes it all the more laughable in its incongruence. Or the artist may make the human being appear

funny in its human-all-too-human aspects, and this human being may in turn make the artist tragic by foiling his aspirations by means of his inherent—comical—weakness, as in Gerhart Hauptmann's tragicomedy *College Crampton*. Other examples are Angelo in Shakespeare's *Measure for Measure* (which as a whole is not a tragicomedy), Schiller's *Turandot*, Georg Büchner's *Leonce und Lena*, Lorca's *Amor de Don Perlimplín*, Carl Hauptmann's *Tobias Buntschuh*, Kleist's *Amphitryon* (Jupiter), Victor Hugo's *Cromwell* and *Le Roi s'amuse* (*The King Amuses Himself*), and Harold Pinter's *The Caretaker*. In all of these, a subtle tragicomic fusion is effected without detriment to either the comic or the tragic. These are, on the contrary, identified at virtually every moment, since, whenever the character appears on the stage he is both at the same time: will and unsatisfactory fulfillment, or being and mask, or reality and appearance, and thereby comic and tragic. Needless to add, a character dichotomy can be utilized in tragedy as well. But the tragedian leaves the comic potential of the incongruity unexploited, much as the comedian, conversely, refrains from accentuating the tragic implications when he uses this device.

The discrepancy within a character is not necessarily a single one. If there is a larger number of such conflicting elements in any one *dramatis persona*, that is, if the character is constituted as nothing more than the sum total of his roles, masks, attitudes, and "faces," then, too, the tragicomedian sees a chance for his craft. The person who is an "actor" (either literally or metaphorically) in every expression of "himself," that is, a person who is not really a self any more but a collection of masks and roles draping an ultimate emptiness, can easily be seen in tragicomic light. The best known example is perhaps Jean-Paul Sartre's *Kean* (based on a play by Alexandre Dumas). The literary movement, however, that is particularly and almost exclusively under the impact of this notion (propounded scientifically by Ernst

Mach in 1886) that man is basically no more than an assortment of momentary "states" held together by no coordinating personal principle, is Impressionism at the turn of the last century. And not surprisingly, the loss of the self was made the subject of tragicomedies by the outstanding representative of this movement: Arthur Schnitzler in his almost programmatic "tragicomedy" *Das weite Land* (*The Expansive Land*) and in *Grosse Szene* (*Great Scene*), to name just these. Pirandello, too, shared this specific tragicomic vision of Impressionism, which he formulated in *Il Giuoco delle Parti* (*The Rules of the Game*).

Finally, there is within this group of devices based on the character structure of the *dramatis persona* the one that, unlike the other two, does not exploit internal dichotomies but rather constitutes a character who is distinguished by just *one* dominant trait. This is exaggerated to such a degree that it makes the person comic and tragic at the same time. In principle, this device of the one (and only one) characteristic exaggerated beyond the norm is, of course, familiar from the comedy of manners or the older comedy of humors, which abounds in such comic types as the miser, the braggard, the bigot, etc. In fact, more often than not, the laughter these types arouse is derisively satirical and is meant to be. In order to achieve *tragicomic* rather than comic effects with this technique, the dramatist will have to modify and transform it in two ways. For one thing, whereas the character traits exaggerated in the comedy of manners are invariably small vices, the author of tragicomedies will have to choose a character feature that is, in itself, a virtue. Secondly, while the comedian does not invest his "types" with human depth and richness of character, the tragicomedian needs to go beyond the merely two-dimensional, poster-type portrayal that befits the writer of the comedy of manners. If he does not do so, he fails to create that human worth and substance that alone makes dramatic figures potentially tragic. A good example of this kind of tragicomic characterization is Tellheim in Lessing's *Minna von Barnhelm*. His sense of honor (which, to be sure, is not a superficial conventional concept but, rather, a demand of his conscience) is exaggerated in such a way that, on the one hand, it appears in intensely comic light while, on the other, it envelops Tellheim in the unmistakable hue of tragedy since his gentleman-like insistence on his honor (in the sense of decency) causes him, throughout the play, extreme suffering, anguish and despair and brings him to the verge of suicide. His sense of honor demands of him a self-denial and refusal of happiness that is profoundly tragic but appears only in the light of comedy. Small wonder that some critics have viewed Tellheim as a purely tragic figure, others as a purely comic one. As one might suspect, this is not a question of either-or. It will also be remembered that Lessing (only a very short while after completing *Minna von Barnhelm*) expressed his belief that the "impossible" identification of the comic and the tragic was, indeed, possible. The device that Lessing used to bring about this synthetic effect was later to become a particular favorite of the Expressionists. With them, it even gained a certain significance in intellectual history, above and beyond its significance in the history of drama, for what the Expressionists show in the light of tragicomedy is the "new man," the human "regeneration," that the movement had hailed so enthusiastically as the panacea to end all contemporary woes, including those that stem from the human condition per se. Expressionist tragicomedy is, thus, an expression of the painful awareness of the failure of a program that had meant everything—but of an awareness that is not blind to the ludicrous aspect of its original presumption. In English literature John Galsworthy's *The Pigeon* (called tragicomedy in a German translation) may come to mind, although it is far from a perfect realization of this structural scheme. Amanda Wingfield in Tennessee Williams' *The Glass Menagerie*, however, is created by a clever utilization of this device. One might also think of Gregers Werle in *The Wild Duck*. One of the most perfectly realized examples is F. Crommelynck's *Le Cocu Magnifique*.

These are the most important techniques by which tragicomic effects can be achieved. It is not at all unusual to find two or more of these, rather than just one, used in one and the same play. Moreover, the "narrative" method of dual *point-de-vue* discussed at the outset of this section may be introduced in a tragicomedy in order to sharpen our eyes for the perception of the more genuinely dramatic techniques. And their plurality in one and the same drama, which is the rule rather than the exception, is indeed often a matter of necessity rather than choice. If, for instance, the tragicomic *changeant* is to be lent to a play which has several major figures instead of just one, it is obviously expedient to use more devices than one.

An Aside on Method: The Hazards and Rewards of Genre Studies

The structural devices discussed in the previous section emerge from a comprehensive study of the history of the genre, tragicomedy. But how does one, how can one study such a genre and its history?

One point is clear (though it adds to the complications): neither the aesthetician nor the historian of modern tragicomedy can let himself be guided exclusively by the explicit designation of plays as tragicomedies. If they did, all they would arrive at would be a survey—typological or historical or both—of what has by different authors at different times since the eighteenth century been called tragicomedy. This, however, would be less than mildly interesting. From such a survey, one would learn, for instance, that Henry Arthur Jones in 1907 thought nothing of declaring his social criticism play *The Galilean's Victory* "a Tragi-Comedy of Religious Life in England" and that he probably never thought about the matter at all. One would learn that Michel de Ghelderode wrote a macabre, grotesque play, *Fastes d'Enfer* (*Chronicles of Hell*), and called it "tragédie bouffe." One would learn that Valle-Inclán's cynically disillusioned portrait of human greed, *Divinas Palabras* (*Divine Words*) with its macabre touch of an Irish wake under Castilian skies, was dubbed tragicomedy by the author. Finally, it would be recorded that Arthur L. Kopit's successful spoof of family life, American style, *Oh Dad, Poor Dad, Mamma's Hung You in the Closet and I'm Feelin' So Sad*, bears the subtitle "tragifarce," and so on. None of these plays is tragicomic, of course.

On the other hand, there is also an abundance of modern plays that are written in the tragicomic mode, although this fact is hidden from the first superficial view by "safe," nondescript labels like drama, play, *pièce*, *Stück*, etc. Sometimes a translation will correct the misleading impression by supplying the more appropriate designation, tragicomedy. Cocteau's "pièce" *Bacchus*, for example, appears as "Tragikomödie" in the Langen-Müller edition of his *Dramen* (1960), and *Waiting for Godot* was called tragicomedy only in the author's own English translation, not in the French original. Labels, in the advertisement business as elsewhere, are not always designed to provide information. Some are outright misnomers. Thus, Gerhart Hauptmann subtitled his *College Crampton* a "comedy" but acknowledged later, and rightly so, that the play was, in fact, a tragicomedy. And Ibsen termed *The Wild Duck* a tragicomedy although in the original subtitle it had simply been called a play. Even so, a good many modern dramas, designated as tragicomedy or tragical comedy or the like in the subtitle, *are* tragicomedies in the sense that we have so far used the term. Let us just mention the *Play on Lead-Peter* by the contemporary Norwegian critic and dramatist Odd Eidem, Dürrenmatt's *The Visit*, O'Casey's

The Silver Tassie, Abercrombie's *Phoenix*, Galsworthy's *Skin Game*, Davidson's *Smith*, Werfel's *Jacobowsky and the Colonel*, Ionesco's *The Chairs*, Strindberg's *Creditors*, and some plays by Carlos Arniches.

If the label is not a reliable guide to a grouping of dramas in modern times, what is? Or, is it at all possible, let alone useful and desirable, to classify dramas according to genre? The question is fundamental, and fundamental answers have been given. To start with the most provocative one, J. L. Styan has stated categorically in his *Elements of Drama* that "we can no more judge a modern tragedy by the standards we might apply to Greek tragedy than we could comfortably wear a suit of armour in an underground railway." [39] This may be so (though one wonders about the "standards" applicable to all Greek tragedy and when and where armors were worn comfortably). Apparently, we are dealing with different kinds of tragedy. But does it follow that "a classification of plays by types is today supremely unhelpful; to stamp a play as a tragedy or comedy, a melodrama or farce, is to bind it by rules external to itself and illegitimately borrowed?" [40] The underlying assumption of this view is that whereas formerly the dramatist observed certain "rules" in his production, the modern writer determines the nature of his play by his "particular attitude to his theme and audience, the attitude which gives it its predominant tone." He thereby "exults in his freedom to play over an audience's whole emotional scale" and even to "explore new territories of feeling." [41] As a result, the contemporary playgoer cannot, as he presumably could formerly, "anticipate his response" any longer by consulting the generic subtitle of that drama he is about to view. Again, this may be so. But does it follow that the modern audience must therefore "think of distinctions of quality, not of kind?" Is it not conceivable, on the contrary, that these "qualities," "attitudes," and "tones" can be classified according to kind? Is it not thinkable that several authors will, independently or within the framework of a "school," choose the same "quality," "attitude," or "tone," the tragicomic one, for instance, which surely would allow for ample individual variations without destroying the essential sameness of tone or feeling? It certainly is.

Now, of course, the Benedetto Croce school of literary criticism, which has concerned itself specifically and emphatically with the problem of genre description and genre history, will answer this question without hesitation: the grouping of literary works according to genre is in error because each work, as an expression of the individuality of its creator or of his momentary individual vision, is so unique, so different from every other work that it would be a waste of a critic's labor to attempt a classification according to genre. In other words: the *subject* of all genre studies, be they chiefly historical or chiefly typological, does not exist in the first place; that is, even as an abstraction, genre would be a myth according to this school of thought, which had a wide following, throughout Europe, in the earlier part of this century. For the student of genre, it is a disconcerting opinion to face. It eases his work by showing that it was never there.

But this is a false alarm, for what Croce and his disciples were up against when they took this stand is *passé* for modern genre studies anyway. Not only did they fight Ferdinand Brunetière's biologistic, even Darwinian concept of the development of individual genres in literary history, but the concepts of genre current at the time were dependent "now on outward characteristics, now on content," to quote from Goethe's notes to his *West-Östlicher Diwan:* in other words, dependent on formal characteristics (rhyme, meter) or the criterion of subject matter, or a combination of these. It was demonstrated in the first chapter how such considerations led to the historical concepts of tragicomedy. Today we realize that this approach to genre studies is no longer satisfactory, not only when we deal with modern literary works that were not written in a time when such "rules" had validity to begin with, but also when we deal with "historical" genres such as the sonnet, the passion play, the Jesuit drama: the criteria of "form" and subject matter, we realize, simply do not exhaust the wealth of such works; they touch on inessentials. What more modern genre studies start out with, then, is not the observation of the presence of such formal or material conditions of the work but with what Shaftesbury called "inward form" and has since been interpreted with varying degrees of generosity, though now usually termed "inner form." Modern students of literary genre (Wolfgang Kayser, Günther Müller, Karl Vietor, etc.) proceed from the observation and isolation of distinct aesthetic phenomena—such as the tragicomic—and try to understand how this phenomenon (which is present, first of all, in the tragicomic vision of the author) is realized in the particular organization and articulation of the work of art, which in turn suggest to the reader or audience a tragicomic vision corresponding to the author's.

Thus, modern genre studies start from something which is more basic than certain elements of form and classes of subject matter or types of themes. In proceeding from a specific "vision," they do, in fact, take their departure from an underlying general attitude towards reality, a mode of confronting life in general. This may be either the author's "philosophy of life" or it may be merely one of several possible "attitudes." At any rate, it is from this general vision that the structural devices that were discussed in the previous section are chosen, consciously or instinctively, by the author. The history of the genre of tragicomedy shows that there is indeed a limited number of well-defined techniques which are used again and again by authors of tragicomedies. They emerge as the morphological "constants" of the history of the genre. They exist, of course, only in specific and individual variations, not in supposedly ideal or typical realizations. If one closes one's eyes to this fact, one risks a serious distortion of the total—historical and typological—picture. If one were to select only one or two putatively "perfect," model realizations of the tragicomic and then view the history of the tragicomic genre from this absolutely normative vantage point, one would, at best, write a history of those particular devices of tragicomedy, but not of tragicomedy. The fact is, however, that the same phenomenon can objectify itself in rather different molds. And it is the sameness of the phenomenon, not its specific structural materializations, that determines what belongs to one genre.

Nor is it advisable, as we intimated earlier, to start a genre investigation of this kind with a *normative* description of the underlying phenomenon itself. This would indeed be impossible. In all such studies we are faced with the *circulus* that, to use our example, on the one hand, it is only the history of tragicomedy that tells us what tragicomedy and the tragicomic are while, on the other hand, such a history of tragicomedy can be viewed and written only with an awareness of what tragicomedy and the tragicomic are. This, in turn, we can only learn from the history of the genre, which in turn. . . .

But this circle is not necessarily vicious, for our hypothetical (and expediently vague) idea of "the tragicomic" did not spring from a vacuum, but from familiarity with tragicomic works. Therefore, this idea is not a normative definition but what Vietor, the pioneer of modern genre studies, calls a "Vermutungs- und Ahnungsbild," [42] that is, a tentative and intuitive image. This intuitive idea may lead us to the identification and appreciation of other tragicomedies, and, as it does so, it is further corrected, expanded, modified, refined, and validated. And vice versa, a given work of art may yield its secret charms only when it is approached with an adequate vision of this kind. The critic and historian must, therefore, constantly try to keep in mind the indi-

vidual work and the genre, the part and the whole. In this
fashion, "by synopsis of all individual works belonging
to the genre," he eventually gains a satisfactory notion
of the genre as such. This, then, would be the "abstraction, that is, the conceptual, schematic determination of what is the fundamental shape, the 'universal' of
the genre that exists only in so many individual cases." [43]
(That there are borderline cases is to be expected; literature rarely allows itself to be compartmentalized too
neatly.) This is the basic agreement of all modern students of literary genre.

But let us now return to our more specific problem,
the tragicomic genre in drama. If literary genres are, as
stated above, ultimately and basically a matter of a particular "vision" or a general attitude towards life and the
world, this is perhaps most patently true of the tragicomic genre. Modern critics as well as authors of modern tragicomedies, especially those of our own day,
usually make this point. It is, in fact, one of the most
important to be made about the genre. Tragicomedy, it
is asserted almost with regularity bordering on monot-
ony, is the only adequate expression of the human condition as seen in the "present." But what exactly are
these philosophical and anthropological implications of
the tragicomic vision? What is the meaning and significance of the tragicomic mode that is so prominent today? And why is it so prominent today? In attempting
to answer this question (in the next chapter), we may
be able to throw some light, however dim, on the intellectual physiognomy of man in our time.

CHAPTER

III

The Meaning and Significance of Modern Tragicomedy

DELMONTE: *I play everything, classical and modern plays, tragedies and comedies.*
ISABELLE: *And you never get them muddled, mix them up at all?*
DELMONTE: *Never used to in the old days! Comedy was comedy and tragedy was tragedy! But with the plays we get served up nowadays, of course. . . .*
JEAN ANOUILH,
Dinner with the Family
(tr. by Edward Owen Marsh,
1958, p. 58).*

The "Modernity" of Tragicomedy

In 1899, Alberto Cantoni the Italian humorist, in one of his essays, has what he calls classical and modern humor confront one another in the guise of a rubicund and jo-

* By permission of Methuen & Co. Ltd., Publishers, and Dr. Jan van Loewen Ltd.

vial old man and a slender, circumspect little fellow
with a taunting expression on his face, respectively. In
their argument about their relative virtues, the little one
reproaches the older man for being vulgar and inde-
cently sensual, whereupon classical humor replies to
modern humor: "As a result of your constant repetition
that you seem to smile, but are suffering . . . it has
happened that nobody knows any more what you really
seem and what you really are. If you would see yourself
you would not know . . . whether you rather weep or
smile."[1] This sounds like negative criticism; but, as
such, it is purely ironic, and there is no doubt as to
whose side Cantoni is on. Nor should one doubt that he
means to say that the comic in modern times has a distinctly tragic undertone, or, vice versa, that the tragic
tends to express itself in the hue of comedy. While in
"classical times" the comic and the tragic were separate,
they have become inseparable, in fact, indistinguishable
in the modern age, the little fellow goes on to say, and
Cantoni agrees. Certainly, this brand of "humor" would
find the best conditions for its realization in drama.
This, of course, would be tragicomedy.

   Pirandello, one of the most outstanding champions of
tragicomedy in our time, quoted Cantoni's argument in
favor of "modern humor" in his *Umorismo* of 1908, ap-
proving the basic point the "critico fantastico" was
making. There is, indeed, no lack of authors and critics
who argue in a similar vein. The point they make over
and over again is that tragicomedy (in the sense of the
word that we have so far developed) is a particularly or
even uniquely appropriate expression of the temper of
the "present." Thomas Mann, in his preface to the German translation (1925) of Joseph Conrad's novel *The
Secret Agent*, even went so far as to assert that "broadly
and essentially, the achievement of modern art is that it
has ceased to recognize the categories of tragic and
comic or the dramatic classifications, tragedy and comedy, and views life as tragicomedy."

Two separate assumptions are contained in this statement which has been expressed similarly by so many writers from Victor Hugo to Ionesco; first, that tragicomedy is a literary genre which implies and objectifies a view of the world that is deemed to be especially profound and expressive of the human condition; and secondly, that this genre is a distinctly modern achievement. Let us begin with this second assumption and analyze the imputed *Weltanschauung* later.

The trouble with the well-nigh ubiquitous claim for the modernity of tragicomedy (in the synthetic sense of the word) is that it is only rarely clear what is meant by the modern period. One glance at the repertory of metropolitan theaters anywhere in the western world would quickly convince us, to be sure, that the view that tragicomedy is a specifically modern genre holds true for the present. But the fact is that similar assertions have been made since the latter half of the eighteenth century although it is not known just how close these critics looked at what was actually performed on the stage at the time.

Not surprisingly, such assertions are often made by those critics who are eager, and sometimes all too eager, to write out a death certificate for tragedy as commonly understood until that particular moment in literary history. In our own time, the "death of tragedy" has all but become a household phrase, and there are so many mourners at its bier that one wonders how it happens that even now so many plays are sent out into the world proudly bearing the time-honored title of "tragedy." The point is, of course, that only the traditional and, to most critics, canonical variety of tragedy has disappeared almost completely in our time, namely that tragedy which presupposes an essentially unshakable metaphysical world order instituted by the supreme powers variously called god, gods, fate, providence, or the like. Wherever this normative framework of ultimate reference loses its power of conviction or is willfully discarded, so it is believed, the traditional tragic hero disappears as well, and with him, tragedy. As a result, man is no longer seen in his relation to God or some metaphysical realm which invests him with dignity but, rather, as a victim of his psychic determination and social condition. And if under these auspices he does fail "tragically," he does no longer fail *sub specie aeternitatis*, before god, but falls prey to a "fate" which is nothing but the ever so complicated interaction of factors explicable in biological, psychological, and sociological terms. In other words, the theological dimension of tragedy is lost; the dramatic god is dead; man as a purely psychic and social being no longer commands the reverence he used to command *sub specie aeterni*. Arthur Miller, to mention just one of many, formulated this almost commonplace view of the contemporary malaise with particular cogency.[2]

The result is plays like *Mourning Becomes Electra*, *Death of a Salesman*, or *A Streetcar Named Desire*, purely social and psychological "tragedy," so-called naturalistic tragedy, which usually ends on a note of despair unrelieved by the silver lining that appears in the metaphysical reconciliation and religious assurance of traditional tragedy.

Comedy, of course, would seem to be untouched by this development in its sister genre. Or is it? We might well ask this question since, much like tragedy, comedy too presupposes a certain normative concept of a world order which is unshakable and absolute—otherwise it would hardly be possible for the audience to maintain its stance on the vantage point of relative security from which the events can be appreciated as comic. They are comic because they conflict with whatever "standard" of behavior or attitude is presupposed as the norm. As Leonard Cabell Pronko reminds us, "in a universe without absolutes tragedy is impossible. In such a universe comedy is no longer possible either for man seems to belong nowhere, is the constituent of no hierarchy, either divine or social." [3] If, then, comedy requires, of the author and of the audience, the same certainty about the existence of a normative order that tragedy demands, how is it to be taken for granted, as it frequently is, that comedy was entirely unaffected by the loss of those ultimately religious norms which constituted an essential element of traditional tragedy? The awareness of a norm, no matter how loosely defined, is, as we demonstrated in the chapter on the theory of tragicomedy, a *sine qua non* of the perception of the tragic and the comic alike. If, then, the norm fails to suspend our disbelief, it follows that both comedy and tragedy should be affected. And indeed, a modern drama critic, Travis Bogard, attributes the dearth of tragedy and comedy in our age to the fact that both genres are "alike in their central point of view and their final assertion," which is an "affirmative assurance of life's lasting fulfillments," which in turn is a testimony whose nature is, in the last analysis, religious.[4]

An idea suggests itself at this point: Is it conceivable that this double loss should, paradoxically, result in a singular gain? Conceivable or not, this is indeed the case, for it is an indisputable historical fact that the decay of both tragedy and comedy is paralleled by a spectacular rise of the mixed dramatic genres, the most exquisite of which is tragicomedy.[5] By some strange process of aesthetic alchemy, the tragic sense of awe is felt again in this hybrid genre, and so is the irresistible appeal of the comic. Whether we witness a performance of Dürrenmatt's *Visit*, Ionesco's *Chairs*, Anouilh's *Colombe*, or Pirandello's *Henry IV*, it is invariably this complex double awareness that determines our reaction to the events and persons on the boards. Christian Morgenstern's provocative paradox that "tragedy is the highest form of comedy," [6] does indeed gain some concrete meaning in the modern theater.

Tragedy, we find, appears in the mask of comedy; and, conversely, as a recent critic has remarked on the development of comedy in modern literature, "we discover that the very basis of comedy is tragic." He continues: "Indeed, the modern playwright no longer cares to separate his worlds into tragedy and comedy but prefers to use the term tragicomedy or, like Brecht, omit any designation altogether." [7] And this is not merely a matter of labeling, for the very themes and problems on which tragedy used to pivot in earlier days seem to have been usurped to a considerable extent by what ironically calls itself farce in our own time—ironically, because it is farce in the sense of Ghelderode's subtitle to *Pantagleize:* "vaudeville attristant," a farce that makes you sad. In other words, while in what is left of "tragedy" and "comedy" the religious framework of orientation is either deliberately broken down or crumbling due to its own inadequacy, the modern tragic farce of Beckett, Ionesco, Dürrenmatt, and others often concentrates on man *sub specie aeterni* and asks those ultimate questions concerning the nature of man and his position and significance in the universe which, in earlier ages, were the exclusive domain of tragedy. Therefore, in an inexplicable and oblique way, the loss of transcendence which we observe in tragedy is frequently canceled in modern tragicomedy. As a result, modern tragicomedy becomes, in effect, that kind of metaphysical drama that tragedy used to be in its better days. Significantly enough, Ionesco, in developing his theory of modern tragic farce, complains that the comedies of Molière were too "unmetaphysical" since, unlike Shakespeare's plays, they failed to raise "questions about the whole condition and destiny of man." This, however, is precisely what Ionesco, according to his own self-evaluation, attempts to do in his own farces.[8] And he may well be right. Is it a coincidence that the only words that the orator produces at the conclusion of *The Chairs* are "à Dieu"? Can the more or less overt references to a mysteriously capricious and, to all appearances, cruel or even cruelly amused supreme being be entirely overlooked in Dür-

renmatt's or Beckett's tragicomedies? In the plays of
Frank Wedekind, who has been acclaimed as one of the
most influential forerunners of the present-day theater
of the absurd, this notion of the sadistically amused god
presiding over a tragicomic world is already present,
most grippingly so in *Musik* of 1906. It has been said
even about Claudel that his "universe appears as a comedy that God puts on for Himself." [9] And concerning
the dramatist Armand Salacrou, the remark has been
made that the God of his dramatic universe is amused
by the struggle of the "free man" and that "on the
whole the anxiety created by his theatre is . . . metaphysical," reminiscent, in fact, of Pascal's fright of the
universe.[10]

One of the first to perceive this trend toward metaphysical tragicomedy (advocated, but not realized, by
the early German Romanticists) was William Butler
Yeats who was convinced that all European literature
after Alfred Jarry's *Ubu Roi* (1896) was going to be
dominated by the image of the "savage God." [11] Various
modern critics have testified to the fact that Yeats was
not mistaken. Thus, George E. Wellwarth states that
" 'the comedy of the savage God' might almost be a
catch phrase to describe the whole avant-garde movement." [12] Similarly, Pronko observes about the modern
experimental theater in France that "those who are the
most hopelessly pessimistic and the most clearly 'metaphysical' are often the most laughable." [13] Recent critics
have spoken variously of "cosmological comedy"
(Ruby Cohn), "metaphysical farce" (Rosette Lamont),
and "ontological comedy" (J. S. Doubrovsky) when
talking about these savagely cruel gods who, as in Cocteau's *La Machine Infernale*, seem to preside over much
of present-day tragic farce.[14] Now, Yeats' assertion was
certainly all too generous; but we may well ask if the
place and function that god had in traditional tragedy
has not been taken over by a fascinatingly enigmatic
Godot in modern tragicomedy.

Yet again: how modern is modern? When does the appeal of the tragicomic mode begin? Surprisingly enough, it has its inception much earlier than the recent pronouncements cited so far may lead us to suspect. A brief flashback is, therefore, in order before we return to the writers of our own century.

The first to proclaim tragicomedy (in the synthetic sense of the word) as the modern dramatic genre par excellence were the Romantics, in Germany especially, but in France as well, while the English Romantic writers were less inclined to indulge in this kind of generalization. Ironically, however, it was an English dramatist, Shakespeare, who did most to encourage the continental critics and philosophers to make precisely these sweeping statements. This does not mean that they interpreted all or even a selection of Shakespeare's plays (such as the so-called "dark comedies" which some critics unfortunately lump together with tragicomedy) as consistently realized tragicomedies, although, of course, a good case could be made for some of them. Rather than that, they observed—much like some progressive neoclassicist critics—that Shakespeare did bring about an intricate fusion of tragic and comic moods in various more or less isolated passages throughout his plays, and —unlike the neoclassicists—they maintained that these were the genuine hallmarks of "modernity" in literature. F. W. J. Schelling, the German philosopher, insisted professorially in his *Philosophie der Kunst* (*Philosophy of Art*, 1802-03) "that the mingling of opposites, that is, above all of the tragic and the comic itself, is the basic principle of modern drama." [15] And by this he does not mean a mere juxtaposition of the extremes but a blend in which the comic and the tragic do not weaken but, maintaining their innate qualities, strengthen each other. Modernity, in these contexts, is usually tantamount to "Romantic." Thus, E. T. A. Hoffmann, to mention just one, stated that "only in the truly Romantic do the comic and the tragic mix so intimately that both melt together in a total effect, moving the feelings of the spectator in a uniquely strange manner." [16]

At first glance it may seem arbitrary to single out this particular feature of the Shakespearean world or, more generally, of modern literature as more significant than its many other aesthetic peculiarities. The reason for this choice is, however, that the fascination which the tragicomic exerted was not primarily aesthetic at all, but philosophic: That man can view himself as comic and tragic at the same time; that he can even conceive of the universe as a metaphysical tragicomedy in which he is a tragicomic *dramatis persona* with god, or, more romantically, the "spirit of the world," as the author, or, at any rate, the producer—this was, for the Romantics, not so much an achievement of the artist as a spectacular feat of the philosopher. Most German Romantics were thrilled by it. And, as one might expect, they were quick to theorize just why this "extraordinary philosophy of life," as Heinrich Heine called it (*ungeheure Weltanschauung*) in a letter to Friederike Robert of October 12, 1825, had become a distinct possibility only in their time, with Shakespeare as a lone and previously unrecognized pioneer, who "characterizes the spirit of modern literature most fully and most precisely." [17] (The Spanish drama of the Golden Age, the *comedia de capa y espada*, was referred to much less frequently.)

The most unsophisticated stage of this theorizing is represented in August Wilhelm Schlegel's Vienna Lectures (1808), which were soon to win international fame as a result of Madame de Staël's celebrated book on Germany of 1810. Following a lead of his younger brother, Friedrich, August Wilhelm claimed that the tragicomic mode was the most truthful and intimate expression of the mentality of the moderns because this mentality was no longer characterized by harmony and confidence in the healing powers of life, but by contrast and unrest, tensions and disharmonies of all kinds. Thus, the drama of the modern age, as distinguished from the drama of antiquity, *had* to be a "mixed" drama since drama was a genuine expression of the state of mind of the time that produced it. And the most obvious form of mixed drama was, of course, tragicomedy. Even so, the Romantic dramatists themselves did not produce significant tragicomic plays, finding it easier, no doubt, to postulate this difficult genre as the drama of the future.

But even if we set our minds at ease about this point as confidently as the Romantic critics did, we are left wondering exactly why the tragicomic mode rather than any other disharmonious mode should be the distinguishing trait of the "modern" age. One answer is provided by Schelling's speculations on cultural history, with which A. W. Schlegel was familiar but did not exploit for his theory of the history of tragicomedy. The reason the dramatists of antiquity had been able to separate tragedy neatly from comedy was, Schelling believed, based on their *Weltanschauung:* If a dramatist is guided by the conviction that some inexorable, supernatural and extramundane fate determines everything that happens in human life, then he will find no room in his serious plays for those incidents that strike us as comic. Once this view is discarded by the dramatist, however, fate, the one and only cause, is replaced by the interaction of various causalities which are all immanent rather than transcendent. In other words, what one loosely terms fate becomes a matter of character and of all the unpredictable circumstances and coincidences as well as of the causal necessities of life. This multiplicity, however, allows the dramatist to introduce the comic along with the tragic since such is the quality of life. Unfortunately it remains Schelling's secret how his view of modern mixed drama as an expression of the putative post-antique awareness of a multiplicity of causes can be reconciled with the fact that this "modern" drama, as Schelling knows, is the drama of the *Christian* era which, by no means, sanctions this atheistically naturalistic view of tragedy, but, on the contrary, retains, though essentially transformed, the notion of the one causative metaphysical force of tragedy. Schelling does not even discuss this problem.[18]

Friedrich Schlegel's speculation is even more arbitrary.[19] According to him every culture is the result of the interaction of spirit (*Geist*) and nature. But whereas the culture of antiquity was dominated by nature, which made for harmony as the general temper of the time, modern, that is post-antique culture, is dominated by spirit and has not yet reached a state of harmony between spirit and nature. Once again, Shakespeare's drama is the most authentic expression of the post-antique cultural and psychological situation.

Leaving this rarefied atmosphere of the acute, if arbitrary cultural-historical speculation of the German Romantics, we might note in passing that Goethe, though generally condemning Romanticism as a cultural disease of only mild clinical interest, in his later years conceded that the romantic mingling of the tragic and the comic was the trend of the time and that it might be sensible to avail oneself of its "barbaric advantages." [20]

The loudest champion of tragicomedy as the modern "Romantic" genre was, of course, Victor Hugo in the preface to his *Cromwell* (1827). It is probably an odd fact of literary history that this preface caused a far greater stir and exerted a much wider influence than the play for which it was written. It did so because it was at the same time the manifesto of French Romanticism against French Classicism and *the* theory of Romantic drama in France. As such, it is a fanfare for tragicomedy as the modern dramatic genre par excellence. But, as fanfares often are, it is loud rather than clear, for accurate terminological and conceptual distinctions were not Hugo's cup of tea. Nor was logic. He does not unequivocally refer to the "new form" as tragicomedy or even tragicomic, but, nonetheless, that is what he means. This meaning is particularly obscured by the fact that he calls the mixed drama grotesque, but, at the same time, defines it as a mingling of the grotesque and the sublime. These, in turn, he identifies with comedy and tragedy so that the modern dramatic genre that he advocates is, in effect, a union of tragedy and comedy.

Thus, Hugo claims, "We have now reached the poetic culmination of modern times. Shakespeare is the drama; and the drama, which, in the same breath, molds the grotesque and the sublime, the terrible and the absurd, tragedy and comedy—the drama is the distinguishing characteristic of the third epoch of poetry, of the literature of the present day." [21] But Hugo goes beyond the mere statement of his observation. He, too, feels compelled to give cultural-historical reasons for this mixture of comedy and tragedy, which he considers characteristic of modern literature. Like Schelling, he attributes it to the advent of Christianity and its image of man. Yet his speculation is entirely different from Schelling's and, it must be admitted, a good deal more convincing since it does not quite lose sight of the pertinent and demonstrable facts: "On the day when Christianity said to man: 'Thou art twofold,'" namely body and soul, "the drama was created." [22] In fact, he points out again and again: the grotesque, the comic, corresponds to "the human beast," the sublime, the tragic to the "soul." He continues: Since man is always both at the same time, beast and soul, it would be an unrealistic abstraction to write comedy and tragedy separately. The reality of man, which is nothing less than the totality of body and spirit, would be willfully ignored. But if the comic body and the tragic soul are to be portrayed on the stage simultaneously, nothing but mixed, tragicomic drama could result. The point which Hugo makes over and over again is that man, being animal and soul at the same time and at all times, is a tragicomic creature since his animality appears all the more comic in contrast with his mind, and the lofty aspiration of the mind all the more tragic by contrast with the ludicrously inadequate body. It is easy to see that both are interdependent: the comic and the tragic mutually presuppose each other. And the historian of tragicomedy will easily recall that what Hugo formulates here, in his slightly inept manner, is really nothing but a familiar device of modern tragicomedy: the dramatic personality made up of two contrasting traits which conflict in such a way that they throw the light of the tragic and the comic on each other simultaneously.

For Victor Hugo, tragicomedy was the drama of modernity and of the future because it was the drama of Romanticism. Curiously enough, for Ibsen tragicomedy was the drama of Romanticism as well as of Anti-Romanticism. In the preface to the second edition of his first play, *Catiline* (1875), "the great silent one" confessed in one of his rare statements on his literary work, that the purpose of all his works to date had been to represent "the tragedy and at the same time the comedy of mankind and the individual." And the details of his description of the tragicomedy of human life are, in principle, not too far removed from Hugo's when Ibsen speaks of "the contradiction between ability and striving, between willing and possibility."

It was left for George Bernard Shaw, however, to proclaim Ibsen as the great initiator of tragicomedy in modern European literature. Possibly taking his cue from Ibsen's own interpretation, he asserted in "Tolstoy: Tragedian or Comedian?" (1921) that "Ibsen was the dramatic poet who firmly established tragi-comedy as a much deeper and grimmer entertainment than tragedy. His heroes dying without hope or honor, his dead, forgotten, superseded men walking and talking with the ghosts of the past, are all heroes of comedy: their existence and their downfall are not soul-purifying convulsions of pity and horror, but reproaches, challenges, criticisms addressed to society and to the spectator as a voting constituent of society. They are miserable and yet not hopeless; for they are mostly criticisms of false intellectual positions which, being intellectual, are remediable by better thinking." [23] One suspects that Shaw praises merits which are in his mind rather than in the work, for he tends to identify tragicomedy and satire. The corollary is that for Shaw the tragicomic genre is merely a temporary and transitional phenomenon of dramatic social criticism which flourishes only as long as "better thinking" is not yet widespread.

But if the reason for the accolade is questionable, the accolade itself is not. For several of Ibsen's best-known plays have time and again been hailed as the consummate realization of the tragicomic mode in drama, and rightly so. This is, however, especially true of the play that is often considered his finest achievement, *The Wild Duck*. In fact, the author himself referred to it as a tragicomedy at one time,[24] and most modern critics have followed suit. Puzzlement at the strangely elusive quality of the emotions aroused by this play has, from an early date, given way to increasing admiration for its skillful blend of the tragic and the comic. To nobody's astonishment, Shaw was among the first to perceive this. Writing in the *Saturday Review* in 1897 he said:

Where shall I find an epithet magnificent enough for *The Wild Duck!* To sit there getting deeper and deeper into the Ekdal home and getting deeper and deeper into our own life all the time, until you forget you are in the theatre; to look on with horror and pity at a profound tragedy, shaking with laughter all the time at an irresistible comedy; to go out not from a diversion, but from an experience deeper than real life ever brings to most men, or often brings to any man: that is what *The Wild Duck* was like last Monday at the Globe.[25]

The surprise has worn off today, but Shaw's view is still shared by many. Nowadays *The Wild Duck* has become the textbook case of modern tragicomedy, "unparalleled anywhere in its mixture of tragedy and humor." [26] Undoubtedly this interpretation does justice to the intention of the author.

Shaw himself was much more dogmatic than Ibsen when it came to stating that tragicomedy was the only literary form that was distinctly modern. Though he, too, like so many others, conceded that Shakespeare was a worthy ancestor, he dated the period of its flourishing "after Dickens," citing especially Tolstoy's *Fruits of Culture* and *Light Shining Through Darkness* as outstanding pre-Chekhovian examples of comedy "more tragic than a catastrophic tragedy" ("Tolstoy: Tragedian or Comedian?"). Having expressed his high estimate of the genre, it is hardly surprising that he claims his own plays follow the pattern of tragicomedy. "I deal in the tragi-comic irony of the conflict between real life and the romantic imagination," he announced in 1905 in the preface to *Major Barbara*. What he meant was, as he had already clarified in the foreword to *Plays: Pleasant and Unpleasant* (II, 1898), that he intended to show the "sometimes terrible, sometimes ludicrous" consequences of living by ideals suggested by overwrought imagination and clearly out of line with the real nature of man. Again, the tendency to satire makes itself felt, and, according to this reasoning, tragicomedy some day would become a relic of a curious past that could not yet avail itself of the results of a "genuinely scientific natural history."

Shaw's views have a familiar ring: they remind us of what European Naturalism tried to achieve in the wake of Ibsen and Strindberg who both "dealt in tragi-comic irony" as Shaw imagined he did himself. For the Naturalists, though their literary theories were never formulated coherently, the tragicomic was indeed one of the elements of the *moderne* whose outstanding champions they thought they were. "The tragicomedy of human existence," said Troll-Borostyani in an essay on Zola, was the only proper subject matter for the up-to-date Naturalist.[27] But why? The Naturalists charged that literature had, up to their time, applied a one-sided principle in its selection of subject matter. To be represented adequately, reality had to be seen in its infinite variety. Above all, this variety included contrasts of all kinds, of the ugly and the beautiful, greatness and smallness, and, particularly, the tragic and the comic. Thus, tragicomedy, though not necessarily synthetically tragicomic drama, was, once again, a "modern" form.

Whether the Naturalists succeeded in writing this kind of work, is, of course, another question. One might think of some of the mixed dramas of Arthur Wing Pinero with their touches of satiric ludicrousness in the midst of a tragic situation (*Iris*, *The Notorious Mrs. Ebbsmith*, *The Profligate*, and *The Second Mrs. Tanqueray*), or of Hermann Sudermann and the early Gerhart Hauptmann and Leo Tolstoy (though not his most important naturalistic play, *The Power of Darkness*), and finally of the Polish Naturalist Gabryela Zapolska (*Panna Maliczewska*, 1912). Yet it remains doubtful whether the Naturalists lived up to their own expectations. Nor could they, as they were by and large more interested in social criticism than in the art of literature.

One might conclude from the manifestoes analyzed so far that the advocates of tragicomedy as the modern genre par excellence, make up a rather mixed company. And it gets even more mixed if we look ahead of European Naturalism. As pointed out in the previous chapter, Impressionism found a strong appeal in that fusion of emotions which is the hallmark of tragicomedy. Walter Pater may have formulated it most gracefully in the opening passage of his *Imaginary Portraits* (1887):

We have had our September Fair in the Grande Palace, a wonderful stir of colour in the wide, open space beneath our windows. And just when the crowd was busiest, young Anthony was found, hoisted into one of those empty niches of the old Hotel de Ville, sketching *the scene of life*, but with a kind of grace . . . which has made trite old harlequin, Clown and Columbine seem like people in some fairy land;

or like infinitely clever tragic actors, who, for the humour of the thing, have put on motley for once, and are able to throw a world of serious innuendo into their burlesque looks, with a sort of comedy which shall be but tragedy seen from the other side.

The particular image of man that suggested the tragicomic reaction to the Impressionists was described as the loss of the "self": Man was no longer a person with a substantially unchanging core of character, but merely a multitude of sense perceptions that were forever in a state of flux. This image of man, however, was felt to be "modern" since it was the view of the human "personality" that contemporary science (Ernst Mach) suggested.[28]

Guillaume Apollinaire "joins the crowd" when, in 1916, he says in the preface to his *Les Mamelles de Tirésias* (*The Breasts of Tiresias*, written in 1903 but not performed until 1917) that he would find unbearable any play in which the tragic and the comic do not confront each other. "For there is such energy in humanity today and in young contemporary literature that the greatest misfortune appears immediately as justified, as capable of being seen not only from the viewpoint of benevolent irony which allows laughter, but also from the viewpoint of genuine optimism which consoles immediately and allows hope to grow." This optimism does, however, contrast strangely with the nihilistic despair that is prevalent in most of the tragicomic "avant-garde theater" of our own day, which frequently claims, not without justification, *Les Mamelles de Tirésias* as its ancestor. But the peculiarly despairing note of avant-garde tragicomedy is clearly audible in another of its forerunners, Frank Wedekind, as well as in the Expressionists who helped rediscover him after World War I. With them, as with all the others discussed so far, the modernity of tragicomedy is a matter of course, though this is implied in the theme of their plays rather than formulated in explicit theory. That is to say, in the tragi-

comic plays of the Expressionists, whether or not
specifically dubbed tragicomedy, it is the typical Expressionistic hero that appears in the cruelly disillusioning
light of the tragicomic: the "regenerated" man, the man
who has broken through to his true essence. From him,
however, the Expressionists had expected nothing short
of a total regeneration of the world.

García Lorca, too, cannot deny his fascination by the
tragicomic mode. Not only do some of his plays, like
Doña Rosita and *Amor de Don Perlimplín*, bear testimony to this fascination, but the author also took pride
in achieving precisely such mixed effects. His brother
Francisco reports that Lorca commented on one of his
plays: "If in certain scenes the audience doesn't know
what to do, whether to laugh or to cry, that will be a
success for me." [29] One cannot help thinking that the
Belgian dramatist Michel de Ghelderode shared this am-
bition although by no means are all of his plays tragicomedies. The play which according to his own testimony in the Ostend Interviews (1951) "set him up" in
1927, that is, *Saint François d'Assise*, his first work for
the Flemish Popular Theater, freely and intentionally
mingles the comic and the tragic, though predominantly
in the form of "alternation." [30] Another one of his best
known plays, *Pantagleize* (1929), is significantly subtitled "vaudeville attristant" which suggests the double
vision of tragicomedy.

The most outspoken advocates of tragicomedy in the
Romance world, however, are the Italian writers, among
them Luigi Chiarelli, Luigi Antonelli, Ernesto Cavac-
chioli, and Fausto Maria Martini, who, from about 1916
to about 1925, form a loose group usually referred to as
the *teatro grottesco*. Its best known and most prolific
spokesman is Luigi Pirandello. "I see, as it were, a labyrinth," he says, even before the movement gets under
way, in the dedication to a collection of short stories
entitled *Erma Bifronte* (1906), "where our soul wanders
along so many diverse, opposing, intricate roads, with-

out finding a way out. And I see in this labyrinth a herm that laughs with one face and cries with the other; in fact, on one face it laughs at the weeping of the opposite face." As Walter Starkie has remarked, these words about the soul of man in the twentieth century may be taken as a symbol of Pirandello's "literary personality" [31] and, one might add, of the *teatro grottesco* generally. "Even in the most tragic moments of our life we are pursued by ridicule," says a character in Chiarelli's *The Mask and the Face;** and Rosso di San Secondo, for instance, the other leading figure in the group, in the preface to his *Marionette, Che Passione*, asserts something rather similar:

What in comedy may seem to be arbitrary, resulting from the torment with which the characters are afflicted, must not give place to the comic, but, on the contrary, to a feeling of tragic humor. Enduring, as in fact they are, profoundly human sufferings—especially the three protagonists of the play —they are like puppets, and their wire is passion. Yet they are still men, men reduced to puppets, and, therefore, deeply pitiable.

This sounds programmatic and is meant to be. The old Romantic notion of the reduction of man to a puppet and life on earth to a puppet show is indeed revived by many of the writers of the *teatro grottesco*, Pirandello included. Along with the maze, it becomes, in fact, one of the key ideas and motifs of the movement. Needless to add, these writers, and especially Pirandello, did not tire of proclaiming the appropriateness of this image of man to the "modern" times, an age of ever increasing mechanization and depersonalization.[32] And as this condition of man is viewed with the dire humor of an almost nihilistic pessimism, tragicomedy, for the writers of the Italian grotesque theater, as for so many others, became that genre particularly suited to an expression of the "modern" temper. As early as 1908 Pirandello, in his

* *International Modern Plays*, Everyman's Library, by permission of E. P. Dutton & Co., Inc., publishers.

book on humor, made himself its most articulate theoretical protagonist.

When the European theater began flourishing again
after World War II, Pirandello was one of the modern
writers who had the greatest appeal to audiences on
both sides of the former front. But, characteristically, it
was not the entire protean *oeuvre* of the Sicilian writer
that held this sway over theatergoers everywhere. It
was, rather, the two works that are most representative
of his *teatro grottesco* and are, moreover, even today his
best known plays the world over, namely *Six Characters
in Search of an Author* (1921) and *Henry IV* (1922).
Of the entire Italian theater of the grotesque, these may
safely be said to have stood the test of time. And there is
something else that distinguishes them from their
group: While not all the works of the Italian *teatro
grottesco* are consistently realized tragicomedies, these
two—unless the *communis opinio* of critics is deceptive
—definitely are. And, in retrospect, it is no coincidence
that it was these that fascinated and continue to fasci-
nate postwar audiences, for there has been a decided up-
swing of interest in tragicomedy as an aesthetically and
philosophically intriguing art form since the last war.
There is, in particular, the "theater of the absurd,"
about which it has been said with authority that its most
distinctive mark is its blend of tragedy and comedy.[33]
There is the phenomenal world fame of Dürrenmatt's
Visit, Ionesco's *Chairs,* and Beckett's *Waiting for Godot,* all of which were called tragicomedy or an equiva-
lent, and rightly so. The names of the authors, it might
be added, are a certain guarantee, if one were needed,
that this fascination with the tragicomic mode is not a
fad or fancy of a fickle audience.

But, to continue, in addition to this widespread re-
vival of interest in tragicomic plays, there have also been
various endeavors on the part of playwrights to demonstrate once again that tragicomedy is the only type of
drama that can cope with present reality in a satisfac-

tory manner, that is, without resorting to one of the many forms and disguises of escapism. And again, as in Romanticism, this is not merely an aesthetic fascination with the tragicomic, but predominantly a philosophic one. These modern critics live up to the question raised suggestively by Julius Bahnsen in the nineteenth century, namely, whether tragicomedy would not really be "the most adequate reflection of the image of the world (*Weltbild*)." [34] They answer in the affirmative. Now and then they even emphasize that this world, overshadowed, as it is, by the mushroom clouds of atomic explosions, the real ones and the imaginatively anticipated future ones of even more cataclysmic proportions, is best expressed in the tragicomic genre. This is suggested, for example, even in such an improbable place as in Anouilh's *L'Hurluberlu* (1959)* when Mendigales expostulates magisterially:

The modern theater has taken a great step ahead. Pure play, simple entertainment is a matter of the past. . . . Temporary inhabitants of this planet threatened by atomic destruction, we have no time for that any more. What matters now is to endeavor to come to grips with the consciousness of man, by man, for man—and in the spirit of humanity. Which does not at all exclude . . . metaphysical anguish and a sort of humor of despair.[35]

As a glance at the repertory of leading theaters, which have not succumbed to the musical, will readily confirm, this statement is largely representative. It implies two things: first, that tragedy, in the shadow of possible total destruction by atomic weapons, has regained its metaphysical dimensions which had become progressively obscured since the nineteenth century at the latest; and second, that this metaphysical tragedy can be viewed, and portrayed with humor, albeit the "humor of despair." Tragicomedy would clearly be the result. While around 1800 Novalis could claim that "after an unfortunate war comedies should be written" and

* By permission of *La Table Ronde,* Paris, France.

while Hofmannsthal could still repeat this after World War I,[36] Anouilh makes himself the mouthpiece of post-World War II writers when he leads his readers to the inference that after a lost war which is also a lost peace, comedies should no longer be written, but, to use a currently fashionable term, only tragic farces. As early as 1923, an otherwise uninspired historian of comedy, Karl Holl, much like the American critic Virgil Geddes in 1930,[37] had ventured a prediction that has indeed come true today, namely, that the comedy of the future would be tragicomedy. But why? Why is it that the tragic has infiltrated comedy more consistently in our time than it ever did before?

In a general way, Thomas Mann—himself, as we noted, intrigued by tragicomedy as *the* "achievement of modern art"—may have provided an answer. In 1954, a year before his death, he confessed in his now famous essay on Chekhov, the Russian tragicomedian par excellence, that the most fascinating aspect of the subject was Chekhov's doubts about the validity of his function as a writer: "Don't I deceive the reader, as I cannot answer the most significant questions anyway?"[38] Thomas Mann was particularly attracted to Chekhov's narrative "A Boring Story," a little piece about an old man who comes to realize that his life has been entirely lacking in meaning. What he replies to a young person asking him "What shall I do?" serves as the leitmotif to the entire story: "I do not know. By my honor and my conscience, I do not know." The old man's plight, the "doubt about the meaning and value of what one does," Thomas Mann feels, is also that of Chekhov and Chekhov's is that of Thomas Mann, and Thomas Mann's is that of the truly modern writer. Or so he intimates. "The Ironic German" was straightfaced for once and may well have been correct in making this assertion. While we are in no position to quibble about details of his interpretation of Chekhov, it is undeniable that, by and large, that is, to the extent that he is not committed to any ideology, Christian or Marxist, nationalist or other, the modern writer is quite aware that he is no longer, as he once was, the conveyer of meanings and, as such, reasonably assured about the justifiability and validity of his mission.

The last European literary and artistic movements to make this claim programmatically for the superior cognitive power of the poet and artist (a claim which was only consistent when it assigned the role of cultural leader and secularized high priest to the *poeta vates*) were Symbolism and Expressionism. Baudelaire speaks for the former school when he says, in his essay on Victor Hugo, that everything has a hidden meaning and significance and that it is the poet who is called upon and qualified to unravel and communicate this meaning. Expressionism hailed the poet even more emphatically as a high priest in a world yearning for meaning after the churches as well as science had disappointed it. But the Expressionist was, it soon turned out, the high priest of a god that failed. Organized barbarity began to sweep over nearly all of Europe soon after, and the trust in the divinatory function of the poet has never since been restored.

Today, the very passion for self-analysis on the part of playwrights and writers is indicative of skepticism on this point. We live in an age of fascinating uncertainty rather than of anxiety, writers presumably more so than their readers. Or else they would not write, for the most important feature of this uncertainty in an age which has raised "absurdity" to the status of a household word of unparalleled consumer appeal is that it extends not only to the assertion that there is meaning but also to the contrary one that there is none. And it is precisely this kind of uncertainty of the modern writer that becomes productive. In the face of the ever threatening possibility of total meaninglessness, the modern writer turns to the almost preposterous endeavor to reflect and realize the world in his work of art, to grasp the ungraspable by making it the subject of his intuition and of his craft. Thus, he does not objectify meaninglessness as is frequently supposed (by partisans of fashionable meaninglessness and their opponents alike). Rather, he challenges what appears to be meaningless, to give an answer to that questioning, to which his writing ultimately amounts. He is, therefore, not the extreme pessimist whom he occasionally fancies himself to be. Instead— mindful perhaps of the common-place observation that the complete pessimist would, in the first place, no longer write any more—he takes up the challenge presented by the threat of meaninglessness. He does so not with the sheer confidence of postwar Pollyannas but with that bravely intelligent hope against hope with which even Thomas Mann's *Doctor Faustus* concludes. He does so with that skeptical "dark hope" and "strange nonetheless" which the German novelist found so universally appealing and true in Chekhov's creative overcoming of his own doubts about his literary creation.

The reason for this small digression on the intellectual situation of the writer in our time is that one of the typical expressions of this particular uncertainty of the modern writer is the tragicomic mode. In it, though not exclusively in it, the modern dramatist can concretize, even if only subtly, that "extraordinary" *Weltanschauung* which Heine saw prevailing in the comedies of Aristophanes. More often than not, modern tragicomedy is what we have called metaphysical tragicomedy. The supreme power that dominates the image of the world created in this drama is the sovereign tragicomedian. God appears as the director of a puppet show who entertains himself with the sufferings of man on earth. The enigmatic god (or fate) of traditional tragedy, who ultimately became a benevolent if severe father, has, in modern metaphysical tragicomedy, changed into the "savage God," whom William Butler Yeats declared to be the patron of modern literature since Jarry's *Ubu Roi.* But even from this nightmarish vantage point of latter-day amateur theology, tragicomedy does not need to be the drama of nihilism par excellence. "God" may show the features of the supreme nihilist, it is true, but even though he is conceived of as an image of the supreme power, of "supreme evil" (Swinburne), of a "providence diabolique" (Baudelaire), a point of orientation is found in what appeared to be a meaningless void. True, this point of orientation makes the abyss of meaninglessness a universe of depressingly negative meaning, of anti-meaning in fact: the "savage God" amuses himself with the suffering of his creatures. Yet paradoxically, as this orientation is established, it can—quite inexplicably but demonstrably—change its significance, from demon to a benevolent *deus absconditus*. In the words of Ariadne in Nietzsche's "Ariadne's Lament": "my only companion, my great enemy."

Tragicomedy, then, is one of the most prominent genres of the postwar theater and the names of its theoretical protagonists that most readily come to mind are, of course, Dürrenmatt and Ionesco. But they are by no means alone, a fact which suggests the representative nature rather than the capriciousness of their analysis of the chances for drama today. Thus, before turning to the profounder and more detailed expositions of the Franco-Roumanian and the Swiss critic-dramatists, it might be instructive to have a glance at similar views held by other prominent living dramatists.

Among them, there is even a figure as unlikely as Christopher Fry. In a little known essay entitled "Comedy," first published in 1950, he makes the point that the modern writer has no choice but to reach comedy by way of tragedy. "In a century less flayed and quivering we might reach it more directly; but not now, unless every word we write is going to mock us." [39] This approach to comedy is, however, not merely a modern possibility according to Fry but a basic capability of the human mind, something that makes it peculiarly human, in fact, and, at present, it is merely actualized more emphatically than at other times. Laughter was born, Fry speculates, when "the human animal, beginning to feel his spiritual inches, broke in on to an unfamiliar tension of life, where laughter became inevitable." * "But how?" Fry goes on to ask. "Could he, in his first un-laughing condition, have contrived a comic view of life and then developed the strange rib-shaking response?" Fry obviously discards this view and gives preference to a different one: "Or is it not more likely that when he was able to grasp the tragic nature of time he was of a stature to sense its comic nature also; and, by the diffi-cult experience of tragedy and the intuition of comedy, make his difficult way?" Under postwar skies, Fry inti-mates, the more perceptive human animals might do well to take cognizance of this nugget of wisdom again. Fry himself is one of those who do. He confesses that when he "sets about" writing a comedy, "the idea pre-sents itself to me first of all as tragedy. . . . If the char-acters were not qualified for tragedy there would be no comedy, and to some extent I have to cross the one be-fore I can light on the other." Remembering some of Fry's so-called comedies, we easily perceive that while they have overcome tragedy, their light is visible only because of the underlying darkness of tragedy that it is focused on, arousing as it does that strange twilight of pensive melancholy mixed with barely subdued joy that is the hallmark of Fry's art. It is this sad, mellowed joy, the author concludes, that is particularly desirable at the present.

There are times in the state of man when comedy has a special worth, and the present is one of them: a time when the loudest faith has been faith in a trampling materialism, when literature has been thought unrealistic which did not mark and remark our poverty and doom. Joy (of a kind) has been all on the devil's side, and one of the necessities of our time is to redeem it. If not we are in a poor sort to meet

* Quotations from Fry in this discussion are from *The Tulane Drama Review*, IV, 3 (1960), 77-79.

the circumstances, the circumstances being the contention of death with life, which is to say evil with good, which is to say desolation with delight.

This contention of Fry's that comedy on tragic ground is the order of the day in our time, sounds, it must be admitted, unusually reassuring, almost calmly serene, when read in this formulation. How unusual this is will become strikingly clear if one compares it with the more anguished tenor of superficially similar notions of writers like Wolfgang Hildesheimer, Karl Wittlinger, Harold Pinter, Jack Richardson, let alone Ionesco and Dürrenmatt. For instance, in Hildesheimer's recent tragicomic play *Die Verspätung* (*The Delay*, 1961) and Karl Wittlinger's startlingly successful *Kennen Sie die Milchstrasse?* (*Do You Know the Milky Way?*), which the author specifically called a tragicomedy in the preface, the tragicomic twilight focused on "our" time and "our" postwar attitudes is a good deal harsher and grimmer than in the moodily melancholy comedies of Christopher Fry. And there is a corresponding acerbity in their theories of tragicomedy as the play for today's audiences. Wittlinger, to be sure, theorized only briefly in the preface to *Kennen Sie die Milchstrasse?* (Zürich: Diogenes, 1961). But Hildesheimer in his Erlangen speech on the "theater of the absurd" sounds a note that suggests a smile with gnashing teeth. He contends that the "theater of the absurd," which he thinks is best represented by Ionesco's not specifically "absurd" "farce tragique" *The Chairs*, is a theater that presents meaninglessness. It asks about meaning and fails to find an answer. The frustration resulting from this dilemma of the modern writer, Hildesheimer suggests, can best be expressed in the tragicomic mode.[40]

The Anglo-American postwar generation, though saved by native level-headedness from overindulgence in the all-encompassing metaphysical and epistemologi-

cal speculations of their French and German counter-
parts, is no less convinced that tragicomedy is the most
suitable type of drama to communicate what is prevailing today. "Everything is funny," Harold Pinter asserted in an interview with Hallam Tennyson in 1960,
"the greatest earnestness is funny; even tragedy is
funny. And I think what I try to do in my plays is to get
to this recognizable reality of the absurdity of what we
do and how we behave and how we speak." [41] Clearly,
Pinter would be hard pressed to tolerate the kind of serene ease that was suggested by his countryman Christopher Fry.

Much the same may be said about one of the most
prominent serious American dramatists of today, Jack
Richardson. The title of a recent play, *Gallows Humor*
(1961), is indeed a telling indication of what he is concerned with. If there is to be laughter, it is to be the
laughter of the condemned man who wisecracks with
the gallow's noose dangling above him. James Thurber,
Richardson extrapolates in the preface to his play,

dealing gracefully with this knotty subject in a recent arti-
cle, made a very useful suggestion to lexicographers and
those who write about comedy. It was that "tragi-comedy"
should be written as one word, without the hyphen and all
of a piece throughout. A simple suggestion but a provocative
one; and by it I believe he means comedy is not something
categorically separated from life's lamentations—something
to be lowered into subplots for relief, a harmless, vapid anti-
dote to the numbing effects of tragedy. Realist that he is, I
believe Mr. Thurber sees all too clearly how life entangles
these two old dramatic opposites without regard to the well-
made play or the Stagirite's compulsion for purity.

What Richardson understands the American humorist to be saying is simply that the identification and
identity of comedy and tragedy is conceivable. Carry-
ing Thurber's analysis a little further, he expresses his
conviction that "comedy, on its highest level, has exactly the same kernel as its opposite—namely, the cele-

brated tragic flaw." This observation then serves Richardson in his endeavor to purge the term comedy of its Broadway connotations "and to hint, that at its best level, the word is far more applicable to *Oedipus Rex* than to *Under the Yum-Yum Tree*." As the reference to Sophocles might suggest, Richardson does indeed see the tragicomic in cosmic and theological dimensions. He refers to them as "whatever fates rule" our "particular world." Tragicomedy, it would follow, is the dramatic genre that is qualified to represent the "particular world" in our day. *Gallows Humor* is an attempt to do just that.

James Thurber, from whom Richardson took his cue, does indeed make extraordinarily high claims for the tragicomic genre in our time. His tenor is, in fact, strangely reminiscent of Romantic manifestoes, unlikely as such a comparison may sound. Vigorously stating "The Case for Comedy" in the November, 1960, issue of *The Atlantic*, he writes:

The true balance of life and art, the saving of the human mind as well as of the theater, lies in what has long been known as tragicomedy, for humor and pathos, tears and laughter are, in the highest expression of human character and achievement, inseparable. Many dictionaries, including the OED, wrongly hyphenate tragicomedy, as if the two integral parts were warring elements that must be separated.

Ionesco and Dürrenmatt, to be sure, are considerably more profound, albeit wordier. Let us try to isolate the core of their advocacy of tragicomedy as the modern drama par excellence.

"To try to belong to one's own time is already to be out of date," Ionesco claims.[42] But this by no means implies that he denies any connection between his drama and his theory of drama on the one hand and the intellectual situation of the *moderne* on the other. Nor does his assertion that the subject of art is the human condition without regard to its social and psychological specifics suggest a disregard for the timely in favor of the timeless as does Antonin Artaud's superficially similar contempt for the time-bound social and psychic realities. While Ionesco does contend that his subject is the *condition humaine* in the most general and basic sense of the phrase, he also insists that his particular themes are genuinely modern. He believes that the viewpoint from which he regards man is particularly suitable at the present time. There is no art which is above its time. Every work of art "springs from . . . a particular time" (149).* He wrote *Rhinocéros* because "forms of rhinoceritis of every kind, from left and right, are there to threaten humanity when men have no time to think or collect themselves; and they lie in wait for mankind today . . ." (151). "Incommunicability and isolation," the author of the *Bald Soprano* goes on to say, "are paradoxically the tragic themes of the modern world, where everything is done collectively." Thus, Ionesco chooses to view the human condition from the vantage point of these peculiarly modern problems, not from a supposedly timeless one. As he does so, the human condition appears to him not as tragic (as the above formulation might suggest) but as "tragicomic," as he indicates in another essay (143). More than that, it is suggested in yet another place (159), the universe itself is tragic and comic at the same time. For Ionesco, the universe does not mean that space which the astronomer investigates but rather what for other ages was the realm of the metaphysical. Ionesco frequently speaks of the "metaphysical." To view man within the framework of this metaphysical dimension is the prime obligation of the dramatist, of the comedian, in fact. This is precisely where, according to Ionesco, Molière failed. Molière does not hold the attention of the cultured spectator simply because he disregarded man's relation to the "metaphysical" whereas Shakespeare did raise "questions about the whole condition and destiny of man,"

* In this discussion of Ionesco's theory all page references in parenthesis are to his *Notes and Counter-Notes* (New York: Grove Press, 1964).

(19) much in the same way that Ionesco tries to do so himself (222).

Conceived of, then, in such metaphysical terms, the universe appears tragicomic to Ionesco. It is tragicomic because it seems to be devoid of meaning. Thus, the theme of *The Chairs*, which was written "to push beyond the present frontiers of drama," that is beyond the frontiers of "ametaphysical" drama, is "the ontological void" (190). And yet, this ontological void seems to be presided over by some capricious god. Ionesco's theory of the ontological void, his theory of nihilism, therefore, occasionally takes on the appearance of that weird negative amateur theology which we know from the continental Romantics and the manifestoes of European decadence. Thus, puzzled by the strange contradictions of life, the French tragicomedian at one point resorts to the suspicion that a god is making fun of man (233). This sounds whimsical. Yet in such statements Ionesco does not at all glory in the pose of supposedly interesting eccentricity, for it is his serious conviction, expressed over and over again at the slightest provocation, that the dramatist, if he takes himself seriously, is capable of conveying "truths" about the nature of man, his destiny, and his place and function in the universe. Indeed, Ionesco insists that the dramatist is the "true philosopher" (36). And it is, then, to this "authentically philosophical insight" (36), not to an arbitrary mood that "the strangeness that seems to pervade our whole existence" (28) appears as tragicomic.

But why should it? The answer is to be found in the word that has become the ubiquitous watchword of postwar dramaturgy: absurdity. It suggests itself to Ionesco in his endeavor to assess the human situation in his time. Human life today is absurd because it is essentially unintelligible, leading the inquiring spirit to a strange "wonder" which is at the root of artistic creation. Ionesco claims that this is his "basic emotional reaction to the world" (215). Faced with the "incomprehensible"

world (186), the mind bent upon cognition is overcome
by a frustrating sense of futility. Questions asked remain unanswered; solutions suggested turn out to be illusions; hope invoked reveals its impracticability. This is
the starting position of Ionesco, the dramatist. Yet unlike Goethe, for instance, to refer to the most famous
earlier case of the malaise of the modern writer who
takes upon himself the mission to convey the answers
that philosophy and theology supposedly fail to give,
Ionesco is no longer able to revere the enigma of the
universe with calm confidence. For him, the unanswer-
ing universe is "unendurable." Still, it is precisely this
unendurable universe that should be the subject of the
drama of the present, of comedy in particular, but of a
comedy that is essentially a tragic farce. Repudiating the
"little problems" of Molière's comedy that could easily
be resolved, he postulates the comedy of the "unendurable." The unendurable, however, is at the same time
"the source of tragedy" as one might suspect from the
foregoing remarks (26). Thus, Ionesco can conclude
with the paradox that is strangely logical: "The unendurable admits of no solution, and only the unendurable
is profoundly tragic, profoundly comic and essentially
theatrical" (20). And a little later on in the same essay
we find the oft-quoted sentences that are the core of
Ionesco's dramaturgy: "For my part, I have never understood the difference people make between the comic
and the tragic. As the 'comic' is an intuitive perception
of the absurd, it seems to me more hopeless than the
'tragic.' The 'comic' offers no escape" (27).

That is to say, the comic in the metaphysical dimension is more depressing than the tragic because the
tragic as traditionally conceived, in all its pain and bitterness, still "admits the reality of fate and destiny, of
sometimes incomprehensible but objective laws that
govern the universe" (27). The tragic, therefore, still
retains a vestige of metaphysical comfort. On the other
hand, the tragic that is comic (which Ionesco postulates

as the more adequate cipher of the human condition of our time) dispenses with this comfort because it dispenses with those "objective laws." Thus, when Ionesco claims that "the comic is tragic, and that the tragedy of man is pure derision" (27), adding that this is why he calls his plays "tragic farces" or similarly, he means that the basic presupposition of these plays is the "meaninglessness" in that metaphysical dimension which he considers indispensible for modern drama. Speaking about the empty lives of the characters in *The Chairs*, he can, therefore, state categorically that "human beings saturated in meaninglessness cannot be anything but grotesque, their sufferings cannot be anything but derisively tragic" (186). To speak of tragedy under the auspices of meaninglessness of cosmic proportions would be an anachronistic presumption. But to speak of comedy would be nothing less since it too is based on the notion of "objective laws" (27). Paradoxically and yet consequently, one can speak only of that Ionescan "comic" which, as an intuitive perception of the absurd and unendurable, is the same as the Ionescan "tragic." With regard to it, the author corrects his assertion quoted a moment ago; one cannot speak even of hopelessness, he says, because in reality this kind of comic "lies outside the boundaries of hope and despair" (27). Hope and despair presuppose *something* that is hoped for, or despaired of. But face to face with the absolute void, both hope and despair become futile gestures. What remains possible, however, is that perception of the "unendurable," which Ionesco, like others, calls tragicomic. It is, clearly, a straining perception, but at its best moments it exerts nonetheless a compelling charm that defies definition and comparison and yet unfailingly enthralls modern audiences.

Friedrich Dürrenmatt's estimate of the hazards and chances of the present-day dramatist is strikingly similar —and yet different in a remarkable way, for while there is the same note of ultimate futility and of the meaning-

lessness of the greater scheme of things in the theory of
the Swiss dramatist, there is also, instead of Ionesco's
smiling self-abandon and resignation, the brave—though
some would say foolhardy—endeavor to counter the
cosmic absurdity of our time with the delightfully old-
fashioned idea of human worth and dignity and of moral
stamina. The Franco-Roumanian atheist and the Swiss-
German Calvinist would, thus, seem to represent, in
spite of their basic agreement, the two extremes of the
tragicomic vision that both consider to be so uniquely
modern.

Dürrenmatt clarified his position in his speech *Theaterprobleme* (*Problems of the Theater*) first delivered
in 1954. It has been said without exaggeration that this
slim volume of deceptively simple observations on the
modern stage and drama "are among the most important
and most essential statements which can be made on the
theater of our time and any time." [43] As such, they
present the most elaborate theory of tragicomedy as the
modern dramatic genre par excellence that has appeared
to date. It has, as a result, become a classic of modern
dramatic criticism by now although it is by no means
cogently and lucidly reasoned but requires instead careful interpretation to fill in the holes left in the argument.
And, what is more to the point, Dürrenmatt's argumen-
tation proceeds from precisely those premises of the intellectual situation of the present-day writer which
were developed earlier in our analysis of Thomas
Mann's essay on Chekhov which, it will be recalled, was
said to elucidate, in an exemplary fashion, the precarious
plight of the modern writer. Though both Thomas
Mann and Chekhov were strongly attracted to the tragicomic, they did not, however, explicitly and logically
derive the appeal and validity of the tragicomic from
this intellectual situation—which is exactly what Dürrenmatt does.

Before he embarks on his speculative venture,
Dürrenmatt, to be sure, makes the claim that, as he tries

his hand at theory for the first time, he is far from peddling any kind of contemporary *Weltanschauung* such as Existentialism, nihilism, or Expressionism. This almost seems to be standard procedure nowadays; even Sartre uses it. At any rate, Dürrenmatt poses as a practitioner interested in the technical problems of stagecraft and dramatic representation rather than in any philosophy underlying his craft. Inevitably, however, he drifts into philosophical discussions, for it is his contention that every dramaturgy is dependent on "a particular world" since drama is the representation of that world. The "world," however, is variable; it depends on its particular moment in history. Or, rather, as there is no such thing as an objective concept of "the world," what one calls "the world" depends on the historical moment in which it is viewed by the dramatist and, hence, on the perspective of the dramatist. Classical pronouncements in the wake of Aristotle notwithstanding, this is the crux of every theory of drama that purports to represent the world "objectively," for whatever it is that is believed to be the objective image of the world of outside realities and the world of spiritual realities, it is viewed by an individual and is, therefore, subjective. This is self-evident. But the corollary of this truism is not necessarily that the representation of the world, because it is inevitably bound to include an element of subjectivity—because it is a representation of the world "as it appears to us" (43)*—is therefore without any validity, devoid of general interest and acceptability. On the contrary, the strong appeal of certain literary works—and the lack of appeal of others—stems precisely from the fact that they do—or do not—sound a note that is widely felt to be representative and exemplary in its significance as an elucidation of the human condition at a particular point in the history of the human mind. With Dürrenmatt's view of the "world" this is undeniably so,

* In this discussion of Dürrenmatt's theory all page references in parenthesis are to his *Theaterprobleme*, Zurich: Arche, 1955.

as his success may indicate, a success which is not only attested by today's sophisticated theatergoers the world over but by the stamp of approval of sound literary historiography and critical evaluations as well.

What, then, is Dürrenmatt's particular creative vision of the "world" which such a large number of people seem to recognize as theirs? What is the human condition "as it appears to" the Swiss dramatist and, as such, promises to be the most suitable subject matter for the tragicomic drama of the present? The world of today, Dürrenmatt contends, lacks form, perspicuity, lucidity, and profile. The great heroes of the past are no more. What for want of a better word is called tragedy in our time is the result of a diffuse interplay of forces which are not only beyond the control but also beyond the understanding of victim and spectator alike. "Wallenstein's power is still a visible power; today, only the smallest part of power is visible, as with an iceberg, the largest part is submerged in facelessness and abstraction" (44). Our world having become anonymous, bureaucratic and unperspicuous, true representatives and tragic heroes have become unthinkable. Like freedom of action, responsibility is no longer concentrated in any one person as it was in the world that classical drama presupposed, but it gets lost in the faceless and nameless mass society controlled by anonymous power. In other words, the world of today has progressively lost its shape or form (*Gestalt*).

This development reaches its peak at the historical moment of the invention of the atom bomb, which makes the already inscrutable power play in the modern world even more inscrutable and the condition and destiny of man even more mysterious and uncanny. "The atom bomb cannot be reproduced in literature since it can be produced" (45). That is, when human civilization has developed to the point where it can cancel itself out and quite possibly cannot prevent its involuntary and accidental self-annihilation either, "our world" has reached the ultimate in incomprehensibility, unpredictability, and shapelessness.

At this point, Dürrenmatt makes a startling assertion: this is a kind of world that tragedy can no longer cope with. What he means is that tragedy as traditionally conceived of cannot dispense with the concept of metaphysical order and meaning, no matter how recondite, which is the source of whatever "shape" the world of our experience may have. The very concept of tragic guilt, indispensable to traditional tragedy, presupposes such an absolute in relation to which it becomes meaningful. "Tragedy," Dürrenmatt says,

presupposes guilt, distress, measure, perspicacity, responsibility. In the helter-skelter [*Wurstelei*] of our century, in this bankruptcy of the white race, there are no longer guilty men, and no responsible ones either. Everybody cannot help it and nobody wanted it to happen. Everybody is really dispensable. Everyone is dragged along and is caught in some rake. We are too collectively guilty, too collectively entangled in the sins of our fathers and forefathers. We are nothing but children's children. That is our bad luck, not our guilt: guilt is only possible as a personal achievement, as a religious deed (47 f.).

Enmeshed in inscrutable courses of events, man is no longer the doer of his deeds, as he once was when he could still conceive of himself as responsible vis-à-vis a metaphysical principle of ultimate order. Somewhat startlingly, Dürrenmatt concludes from this diagnosis of the modern malady that while tragedy is impossible "only comedy can cope with us" (*uns kommt nur noch die Komödie bei*, 48). This seeming *non sequitur* becomes less erratic if we recall that for Dürrenmatt it is precisely this kind of unformed, shapeless world that comedy "presupposes," to use his own favorite term. In fact, it presupposes a world which is on the point of folding up (*am Zusammenpacken*) "like ours" (45). This sounds disturbing—does it mean that Dürrenmatt's theory of comedy deviates from the tacit agreement of

virtually all other dramaturgies, briefly commented on
earlier in this chapter, namely that comedy, like tragedy, is predicated on the assumption that there exists
some order or norm with regard to which something
appears as comic or tragic? Dürrenmatt does, in fact, not
leave this premise, for his pronouncement on the subject
matter of comedy would be incomplete without the understanding that it is the task of comedy not to reflect
the formlessness that is its subject matter, but, paradoxically, to give shape to the shapeless, form to the form-
less. Thus, comedy would be "the shape of an un-shape,
the face of a faceless world" (48).

But how can it without losing what has traditionally
been its character? In fact, it cannot. Comedy that represents "our world which still exists only because the atom
bomb exists: out of fear of it" (48) cannot instill, even
if it tried, a feeling of serenely amused superiority over
the subject. Dürrenmatt seems to sense this and rather
abruptly continues his somewhat twisted turn of
thought by remarking that even though "pure tragedy"
is no longer possible in the shadow of the atom bomb,
"the tragic" is still a distinct possibility not of tragedy,
but of comedy: "We can produce the tragic out of
comedy, bring it forth as a terrifying moment, as an
abyss opening up . . . comedies from which the tragic
arises" (48).

This is one of the most frequently quoted passages
from all modern dramaturgy. Yet frequent quotation
has not brought us any closer to an understanding of its
implications. To begin with, if tragedy presupposes a
world of form and order and comedy a world of chaos
and disintegration, how can the two be logically united
in one and the same literary work? Juxtaposition suggests itself as an easy way out of this dilemma. But,
clearly, this is not what the author has in mind. Perhaps
one should note the distinction between tragedy and the
tragic which Dürrenmatt makes in the passage just
quoted. If tragedy is no longer possible while the tragic

still is, and if tragedy presupposes form and order, then the conclusion is inescapable that "the tragic," unlike tragedy, is not bound to an awareness of order and shape. The tragic, then, would have to mean the experience of human suffering and frustration which, unlike suffering in tragedy, does *not*, in the last analysis, overcome its note of utter meaninglessness by an awareness, however indirect and inexplicable, of meaning and "consolation,"—that is, meaning and consolation which would, in effect, be an acknowledgment of that very order and norm to which tragedy has traditionally adhered. Thus, it becomes clear that "the tragic" and comedy could very well be united in one and the same work representing "our world"; the reason is that both are related to the formlessness and disorder. "Tragic comedy" in this sense (it is the subtitle of Dürrenmatt's *Visit*) would then be the aesthetic objectivation of nihilism (as the term is sometimes used).

Dürrenmatt admits that this conclusion is not without logic.

Now one might be tempted to conclude that comedy is an expression of despair, but this conclusion is not cogent. Certainly, if one sees the meaninglessness, the hopelessness of this world, one can despair, yet this despair is not a result of this world but an answer which one gives to this world, and another answer would be one's refusal to despair, for example, one's resolution to endure the world, in which we often live like Gulliver among the giants. He, too, keeps his distance, he, too, takes a step back who wants to make an estimate of his opponent, who gets ready to fight him or to escape him. It is still possible to show the man of courage (48 f.).

Once again: *how* is this possible? We may well ask this question, for the foregoing should have made it clear that this is not just a matter of choosing one's *dramatis personae* at liberty. What Dürrenmatt implies by his statement is undoubtedly that a non-nihilistic comedy (albeit tragic comedy) is thinkable, though a

nihilistic one is equally thinkable. Since comedy, while
proceeding from chaotic reality, should, according to
Dürrenmatt, still aim at form and order, the idea suggests itself that the form and order of present-day comedy, which is bound to be tragic comedy, is the form and
order of the "man of courage," around whom it is built.
This is, in fact, what Dürrenmatt, omitting the logical
explanation, indicates. He says on the next page that to
him, as a writer of comedy in our age, "the universal"
(*das Allgemeine*) remains forever chaotic, "the world"
remains "something monstrous, an enigma of disaster
with which one must put up." But he maintains, on the
other hand, that there must be no thought of capitulation
in face of this kind of world: "The lost order of the
world is restored in them" (that is, in the men of courage).

The formulation is not fortunate, but what it aims at
is obvious enough: it points to a precarious balance, in
the tragic comedy of today, of chaos and form, of
shapelessness and order. The disastrous chaos of the
modern world remains chaotic, order remains lost. But
it is countered by the spiritual form and order within
the person who courageously faces its meaninglessness
and bears it, much in the same way Sisyphus of the classical legend does, which is, incidentally, one of the genuinely timely rediscoveries of our century. What gives
him the courage to embark on his seemingly foolhardy
venture is not caprice or spite but "the law within"
which makes him human. The comedy, the tragic comedy that results, is therefore curiously ambivalent and
ambiguous: it is a comedy of despair with regard to the
greater scheme of things; yet it is a tragedy of confidence with regard to man who courageously takes this
despair upon himself. And does this "comedy" not suggest the idea that the importance of the greater scheme
of things is dwarfed by the greatness of facing it in all
its meaninglessness? Be this as it may, Dürrenmatt ap-
propriately concludes his remarks about the ambiva-

lence of the modern comic with the casual yet incisive comment that the comic can be "dangerous" but also "demanding" and "moral" (56). If so, the tragic farce could, for once, be called something other than decadent.

Tragicomedy in the Modern Theater

Unlike other writers on the subject, the author does not feel tempted to add his own apologia and recommendation of tragicomedy to this array of favorable pronouncements on the state of health of a fairly young dramatic hybrid. It may well be, as Gaynor F. Bradish claims in his preface to Arthur L. Kopit's "tragifarce" *Oh Dad, Poor Dad, Mamma's Hung You in the Closet and I'm Feelin' So Sad* that in view of the prevalence of pain and disaster in this world of ours, "the tragicomic play has become the contemporary dramatist's finest solution." For us that is not the point. What is of significance to us is *why* so many critics and writers are of the opinion that tragicomedy is the finest solution.

As we have seen, they are all *modern* authors or consider themselves such, modern being roughly the post-Enlightenment period; and they all claim that tragicomedy is the modern genre par excellence.

Or is it? The Australian novelist Kylie Tennant, whose narratives are, to a large extent, informed by the spirit of the tragicomic in the sense that we are using the term in this investigation, has, in several letters to the author, propounded her view that the tragicomic vision is particularly favored by *primitive* peoples. The Australian aborigines, she says, are especially given to viewing the world with one laughing and one weeping eye. The present author has no way of judging in matters primitive. But it may be worth pointing out that Christopher Fry, in a passage quoted above, speculated that awareness of the comic and awareness of the tragic were born at the same time at some early point in the history of primitive man. One has a hunch that a writer like Ghelderode might agree; describing the Belgian poet's drama as an indissoluble mixture of the tragic and the comic, Jacques Guicharnaud called this mixture "primordial." [44]

This is probably a matter of speculation, or else of anthropological research still outstanding. Anyway, what the historian of literature perceives in his backward glance on centuries of drama is not that the synthetically tragicomic vision is an "early" cultural phenomenon, emerging, so to speak, out of the years of infancy of man, but, rather, a phenomenon of "late" periods, that is, periods which interpret themselves to be "late" and consequently as problematical, as times of crisis. Tragicomedy, in our sense of the word, or a theory of tragicomedy (and be it ever so rudimentary in the form of a mere appreciation of tragicomic moments in a given drama) does *not* appear in times (and in literary groups or trends) that, by and large, seem to feel secure within the framework of some belief or program. Security, which admits of no skepticism or feeling of relativity concerning one's own philosophical or theological position, seems to offer little ground for the writing of tragicomedy or even for its appreciation. On the other hand, wherever and whenever such security becomes the object of doubt, the historian observes a certain openness to both: *e.g.*, in those quarters where European rationalism disintegrates under the onslaught of reason itself, in continental Romanticism where skepticism becomes theological in scope, throughout the nineteenth century which self-consciously begins to consider itself "modern," in our own century, and, with particular vigor, in the postwar period. Awareness of and interest in the tragicomic is, hence, a relatively *late* phenomenon in cultural history. This should not come as a surprise. Not all forms of human self-interpretation and awareness are coeval. They are, to a certain extent, concomitants of specific stages in cultural development

—to avoid the, to some, odious term *Zeitgeist*. Antiquity, for example, it has been pointed out by the Danish philosopher Høffding, did not have a sense of "humor" though it did have satire and wit. The macabre, too, most likely does not antedate the Middle Ages. The "joy of grief" is a phenomenon of European sentimentalism and, as such, distinctly datable. Much like the tragicomic, the grotesque as Kayser understands it (though, again, the word is older) is a distinctly post-Enlightenment phenomenon, dating roughly from the second half of the eighteenth century. One could probably add a few more. But little work has been done so far on the history of such phenomena of human self-understanding.

If, now, we fix the *terminus post quem* of the tragicomic as the heyday of European Enlightenment, the difficulty remains that, time and again, since the Enlightenment the prime examples of the tragicomic mode have been provided by the dramas of Shakespeare. (Yeats even thought that "Shakespeare is *always* a writer of tragi-comedy.") [45] This disconcerting fact cannot be interpreted away by the suggestion that Shakespeare himself was possibly unaware of the tragicomic fusion and that he was, instead, merely following his contemporaries' practice of juxtaposing the comic and the tragic. The other possibility of dealing with this flaw in an otherwise neat chronology would be to classify Shakespeare as a forerunner. There are always forerunners. This alternative is equally unsatisfactory. But it can be said in its favor that in the time span between the Elizabethan age and the late eighteenth century, there is no tragicomic literature to speak of, except *Le Misanthrope*.

Yet we should make a distinction in this discussion of chronology: while it is evident that the *theory* of tragicomedy in our sense of the word dates from the latter part of the eighteenth century, it is not quite so clear when the tradition of "modern" tragicomedy begins. In

other words, does the history of post-Enlightenment
drama bear out the predictions, wishes, and judgments
of the theoreticians?

Disregarding Shakespeare and Molière, we may say
that the history of drama lags behind the history of taste
and criticism by several decades. European Romanticism, as already noted, while contributing much to the
theory of tragicomedy, failed to produce tragicomedy
unless we classify Büchner's *Leonce und Lena*, as some
critics do, as a late offspring of Romanticism. Nor did
the wittily stylized *Weltschmerz* of Byronism, the fashionable fad which swept all over Europe at the time,
bring forth a single tragicomedy. Characteristically,
Victor Hugo's own *Cromwell* (in the preface of which
the author developed his theory of tragicomedy as the
drama of modernity) is not successful in precisely this
respect. The uproar it caused began in 1827. But what
about the preceding decades, the period from, roughly,
the middle of the eighteenth century which did, after
all, supply a good deal of theoretical material as well,
paving, in fact, the way for modern tragicomedy?

With the exception of some German plays, there
seems to be no genuine and intended tragicomedy at all.
What held sway over the European stage of the time,
instead, in addition to traditional comedy of manners
and the traditional *haute tragédie*, was bourgeois tragedy
and sentimental comedy. Indistinguishable as they frequently were, they coalesced into *drame*, *Schauspiel*,
drama. This was sometimes even called tragicomedy,
though, of course, erroneously. The truly tragicomic
plays possibly go as far back as Lessing's *Minna von
Barnhelm* (1767), although its appreciation as a consistently articulated synthetic tragicomedy may be more a
matter of historical perspective than present day critics
are able to realize. It is certain, however, that the tradition of tragicomedy dates back to the boldly mixed
plays of the German Storm and Stress writers, in particular J. M. R. Lenz and Friedrich M. Klinger. It is

some of the earlier works of these authors that come to mind in this context: Lenz's *Der Hofmeister* (*The Private Tutor*, 1774, better known now through Brecht's "modernized" adaptation), *Die Soldaten* (*The Soldiers*, 1776), *Tantalus* (1776), and Klinger's fragment *Der verbannte Göttershon* (*The Banished Son of the Gods*, 1777). Looking ahead, we catch sight of Schiller's *Turandot* (1801), a "tragicomic fairy tale" adapted from Gozzi's *fiaba*, and Heinrich von Kleist's tragicomic version of Molière's comedy *Amphitryon* (1807). A little later the tragicomedies of Christian Dietrich Grabbe (*Don Juan und Faust*, 1829), Georg Büchner (to a certain extent *Dantons Tod* [*The Death of Danton*, 1835] and definitely his melancholy transformation of the commedia dell' arte, *Leonce und Lena*, written in 1836) and, finally, Friedrich Hebbel (*Ein Trauerspiel in Sizilien*, 1851) followed in the wake of these pioneers. Still, though the majority of these are fine plays and part of the standard repertory of every German theater even today, it is not an impressive number of tragicomedies that we can list by mid-century. What is more, there seems to be no non-German tragicomedy up to about that time.

Thus, the tradition of European tragicomedy does not really get under way until the second half of the century, reaching its first peak toward the *fin de siècle* and shortly thereafter. Ibsen probably comes to mind most readily, with his *The Wild Duck* (1884), *Little Eyolf* (1894), and in a minor key, *Hedda Gabler* (1890). But even an early play like *Emperor and Galilean* (1873), which Ibsen himself considered his most important work, could be cited in this context. Strindberg called only one of his plays a tragicomedy, namely *Creditors* (1890), but some others, especially *There Are Crimes and Crimes* (1899), could well be claimed for this "modern genre." Knut Hamsun joins the ranks of his Scandinavian countrymen with his bitterly tragicomic portrait of a civilized society that has reached the end of the line, *Livet*

Ivold (In the Grip of Life, 1910). So does, another decade
later, Hjalmar Bergman in at least one play, *The Markurells of Wadkoeping* (1919), a cruelly tragicomic un-
masking of a conspiracy of silence.

In Russia, Chekhov provides the prime example of the
tragicomic mode, while A. N. Ostrovsky's plays (*The
Storm,* 1860, and *The Forest,* 1872) are too muted in
their shades of melancholy to approach, except momen-
tarily, the tragicomic mode. Nor does Gorki's *Lower
Depths* (1903) go beyond occasional tragicomic flashes.
But many are the critics who recognize *The Cherry
Orchard* of 1904 as the most superb example of tragicomedy of all times, although the author insisted that it
was purely comic and rejected any touches of tragedy
which, he thought, were brought out only by other
people's imagination. In this controversy, Chekhov was
surely mistaken—as was Stanislavsky who, after first
reading the play, tried to convince the author that the
title should be tragedy.[46] Together, they were right, of
course, as sixty years of criticism would seem to indicate. But not only *The Cherry Orchard* is tragicomic.
Some of Chekhov's other plays, notably *The Sea Gull,
Uncle Vanya,* and *The Three Sisters,* while not quite as
consistently articulated as tragicomedies, come very
close to being good mixed drama, if one agrees to let the
resigned sadness of the Chekhovian world pass for
"tragic."

In France, the best known tragicomedy of the time
around the turn of the century is, of course, Rostand's
"comédie héroïque" *Cyrano de Bergerac* (1897); in Hol-
land it is probably F. W. van Eeden's *Yisbrand* of 1908,
specifically called tragicomedy in the subtitle; in English-
speaking countries John M. Synge's "tragically hearted
farces" [47] come to mind, not so much *The Playboy of
the Western World* (1907) as *The Well of Saints*
(1905). Shaw, as we noted, would bring up his own
name in this context. The historian of German literature
would think of such works as *Traumulus* (1905) by

Arno Holz and Oscar Jerschke, *Im Chambre Séparée* (1898) by Paul Ernst, *Der Mitmensch* (*The Fellow Man,* 1895) by Richard Dehmel and some plays by Gerhart Hauptmann, Arthur Schnitzler, and Hugo von Hofmannsthal that have already been mentioned. German Expressionism, too, is represented by a considerable number of tragicomic plays. Wedekind, its predecessor, led the way with works like *So ist das Leben* (*Such Is Life,* 1902), later called *König Nicolo* (*King Nicolo,* 1904), and as the movement gets fully under way it follows suit with tragicomedies like Georg Kaiser's *Von morgens bis mitternachts* (*From Morning to Midnight,* 1916), *Kanzlist Krehler* (*Secretary Krehler,* 1922), and *Nebeneinander* (*Side by Side,* 1923), as well as Herwarth Walden's playlets *Weib* (*Woman,* 1917), *Letzte Liebe* (*Last Love,* 1918), and *Trieb* (*Desire,* 1918).

On the stage of the twenties and thirties we find such mixed dramas as Sean O'Casey's *Juno and the Paycock* (1924) and *The Plough and the Stars* (1926), which are frequently referred to as tragicomedies. Then, there is the Belgian Crommelynck, also his fellow-countryman Michel de Ghelderode with his curiously hybrid plays. Most of them are bizarre and macabre, however, rather than tragicomic; *Fastes d'enfer* (1929), as we pointed out earlier, is hardly a tragicomedy, though called "tragédie bouffe" in the subtitle. *Pantagleize* of the same year is dubbed a "vaudeville attristant" by the author and does come closer to tragicomedy. Generally, there is in our view little in Ghelderode's work that could be called tragicomic. Jacques Guicharnaud, however, has said about Ghelderode that his "force lies precisely in that skillful mixture of the greatest horror and the most knockabout farce, a kind of exaggerated Romanticism. One cannot exist without the other, one issues from the other. . . . Ghelderode's theatre indicates a way toward the realization of the 'primordial' drama where tragic horror and the frankest guffaws are indissolubly mixed."[48]

In Italy the *teatro grottesco* flourished during the

twenties with Pirandello's *Six Characters in Search of an Author* and *Henry IV* as its best known tragicomic plays. But the entire theater of the grotesque in Italy, Wolfgang Kayser has stated authoritatively, "aims at tragicomedy." [49] In Spain, the rich production of Ramon del Valle-Inclán includes some "esperpentos" such as *Los Cuernos de Don Friolera.* (*The Horns of Don Friolera*, 1925) and *Luces de Bohemia* (*Lights of Bohemia*, 1924), which some critics would consider tragic farces. *Divinas Palabras* (1920) is in fact called "tragicomedia." Also, among the numerous popular plays of Carlos Arniches y Barrera there are several that are labeled either "tragicomedia" or "tragedia grotesca" in the subtitle, some with justification. Lorca, finally, whom we already quoted as saying that he considered it a mark of distinction if the audience would not know whether to laugh or to cry about his *Doña Rosita*, has a certain affinity to the tragicomic as, in addition to that play, *La Zapatera Prodigiosa* (*The Prodigious Shoemaker's Wife*, 1930) and *Amor de Don Perlimplín* (1931) will readily demonstrate.

In the postwar period there has been a new flowering of tragicomedy on the European and American stage. Late in life, Eugene O'Neill discovered the tragicomic in *A Touch of the Poet*, written in 1946, published in 1957, and an immediate success. A little earlier, in 1945, Franz Werfel, writing in Californian exile, had fashioned a tragicomedy, a "comedy of a tragedy," out of the harrowing experiences of European refugees in *Jacobowsky und der Oberst* (*Jacobowsky and the Colonel*). There is a ring of the tragicomic in some of Tennessee Williams' plays as well. But it is hardly possible to list all the tragicomic plays of the postwar theater. Nor would it serve any useful purpose in this background study. May it suffice to mention just a few prominent names: Giraudoux, *La Folle de Chaillot* (*The Madwoman of Chaillot*, 1945); Anouilh, *Colombe* (1951) and *Ardèle* (1948); Sartre, *Huit Clos* (*No Exit*, 1944) and *Kean* (1953); Cocteau, *Bacchus* (1951). Nothing more need be said about Dürrenmatt, Beckett, and Ionesco. On two other French contemporaries, Guicharnaud has remarked: "Farcical, tragic, or parodic are juxtaposed or mixed in Schehadé's works, just as in Audiberti's." [50] We might in conclusion refer to Harold Pinter's *The Caretaker* (1960); John Osborne's *The Entertainer* (1957); Odd Eidem's *Spillet om Bly-Petter* (1947); Hildesheimer's *Die Verspätung* (1961); and Albee's *Who's Afraid of Virginia Woolf?* (1962). Zuckmayer has incidentally described his latest play, *Das Leben des Horace A. W. Tabor* as in part a "tragicomic ballad."

One play that might escape attention in this context is Wolfgang Borchert's *Draussen vor der Tür* (*The Man Outside*), which was the greatest success in German theaters right after the end of the war and before the beginning of prosperity. It is, as Hans Egon Holthusen saw a long time ago, a rather insipid work of literature, self-pitying in the extreme and juvenile in its petulance. Even so, if one reads it against the grain, so to speak, that is, with the distance that the years and greater balance have afforded us, its subtle ironies emerge and the whole play appears in the light of the tragicomic. And it is hard to say if this tragicomic hue is contrary to the intention of the author. He may well have been a bit more "above" the immediacy of the situation than theatergoers at the time. Significantly, in his other writings he occasionally conceives of the idea of universal, in fact, metaphysical tragicomedy. As he does so he joins ranks with the majority of the writers mentioned in this survey of tragicomedy on the modern stage. That is, he chooses a genre which "is the dominant mode of our ironic age." [51]

Analysis of The Wild Duck

Proclaiming tragicomedy as the truly "modern" genre is one thing; writing one is quite another, as Victor Hugo's case may demonstrate, and an awareness of the distinctly tragicomic qualities as well as of the techniques of creating them is still another. More often than the layman may think, this awareness is not consciously possessed by the author himself (whose conscious intentions may run along entirely different lines). Instead, the critic often has the job of bringing it out. He does so by helping the reader and the spectator savor the aesthetic essence of each significant moment of the play so that its particular tragicomic qualities and the manner used to produce them are appreciated.

As a rule, the critic will find, to be sure, that not each and every moment of the dramatic action will have this tragicomic quality just as it would be impossible to find a tragedy in which each and every moment is "tragic," that is, a realization of the phenomenon of the tragic. Rather, the critic will usually find that it is only at certain points—well but not necessarily evenly distributed throughout the play—that the specific tragicomic essence of the drama becomes clearly appreciated. This finding, however, should not disappoint us or even give rise to the suspicion that a truly tragicomic play is impossible, for it is these moments that set the tone of the entire drama. Moreover, the merely episodic though frequent appearance of distinctly and eminently tragicomic moments in tragicomic plays corresponds exactly to our mode of aesthetic reaction in theater performances in general. We tend to view the action and the persons involved in it in the light of the impression we gain of them at certain moments of heightened intensity. And, to be sure, this light is not only shed on the events to come in the course of the dramatic development, but it works retroactively in the sense that it disposes the audience to understand the previous events adequately by putting them into perspective. The actor performing in such a tragicomic play should ideally incorporate in his manner of presentation throughout the play precisely that tragicomic quality which those heightened moments suggest. If then, the critic's task is essentially limited to pointing out such crucial moments, he describes nothing less than the nature of the viewpoints from which the happenings on stage are properly to be seen.

The majority of the dramas mentioned in our survey of "Tragicomedy in the Modern Theater" have never been analyzed from this angle, though our understanding of them would certainly benefit from such an illumination of their generic character. Ibsen's *The Wild Duck* (1884) is a case in point. Though it has frequently been called the author's masterpiece, interpretations have to date been primarily concerned with, on the one hand, the "problem" or "thesis" of the play and with its symbolism on the other rather than with the characteristic tragicomic mode in which it is couched. But neither line of investigation has yielded satisfactory results, as the practitioners of these two varieties of the craft of interpretation readily admit. It is still hard to understand why Ibsen, while generally insisting on the value of truth and truthfulness as the real pillars of society, should suddenly proclaim in *The Wild Duck* that the actual basis for happiness is a lasting illusion or a "lie"— especially disturbing in view of the fact that in the play preceding *The Wild Duck, An Enemy of the People* (1882), as well as in the one following it, *Rosmersholm* (1886), Ibsen is so explicit about the diametrically opposite thesis. On the other hand, critics are far from agreement on the question of the meaning and function of the symbol of the wild duck, so much so, in fact, that one writer has stated flatly that so many different and incompatible things are brought together, but not held together, by this device that it would be a futile exercise of critical ingenuity to try to pin down the meaning of the strange bird and its purpose in the drama.[52]

Thus, Ibsen was more right than he could have anticipated when he wrote his publisher, Frederik Hegel, on September 2, 1884 that "in any case they [the critics] will find plenty to quarrel about, plenty to interpret." [53] It was more than author's vanity that prompted him to say this, for an unusual amount of thought and persevering energy had gone into the making of *The Wild Duck*, more precisely: into the refinement of the *dramatis personae* and their dialogue. "But now comes the finer revision," Ibsen wrote to Theodor Caspari on June 27, 1884, after the second draft of the play had been finished, specifying this as "the more energetic individualization of the characters and their modes of expression." Curiously enough, this refining process to which the author subjected his material was to a large extent the art of skilfully hiding these very refinements. This is why Ibsen's plays demand such a high degree of concentration on the part of the reader and why each re-reading of a major Ibsen play will open the reader's eyes to new or slightly different aspects of the work, sometimes disturbingly novel, sometimes reassuringly confirming previously vague impressions, but always rewarding.

The aspect of *The Wild Duck* that must be pointed out in the present context promises to be particularly rewarding. One has a hunch that one of the reasons why this play has so consistently been called Ibsen's masterpiece by critics of the most divergent persuasions is its generic quality. Not surprisingly, then, it has almost as frequently been termed the most perfectly realized tragicomedy in Western literature. The earliest critical comments on *The Wild Duck* were, to be sure, strangely at loggerheads about the mood and tone of the drama.[54] While the *Athenaeum* wrote on May 12, 1894 after the English premiere that "the play must be a joke, a harmless, if not very humorous, piece of self-banter, or it is nothing," other early critics, like W. L. Court-

ney and Georg Brandes, spoke of its "pessimistic" tone,
even going so far as to dub it Ibsen's most pessimistic
play. It was then G. B. Shaw, as we noted above, who as
early as 1897 realized the truth of both of these reactions: "to look on with horror and pity at a profound
tragedy, shaking with laughter all the time at an irresistible comedy . . . : that is what *The Wild Duck* was
like last Monday at the Globe"—which is, of course,
what *The Wild Duck* has come to be for most critics
and theatergoers today. Later Shaw even credited Ibsen
with the establishment of tragicomedy "as a much
deeper and grimmer entertainment than tragedy" on the
European stage, and some critics have followed suit.[55]

Among them is Ibsen himself. Not only had he remarked in a general way in 1875 in the preface to the
second edition of *Catiline* that his literary subject matter
was the tragedy and, at the same time, the comedy of
human existence, but he also seems to have been aware
that *The Wild Duck* deserved the label "tragicomedy"
par exellence, more explicitly so than the rest of his
works. To be sure, he chose the nondescript subtitle
"play" ("skuespil") when he published it, but he was
conscious of the fact that this tag designated something
entirely different from what it had previously identified.
"This new play," he wrote to Frederik Hegel when dis-
patching the manuscript on September 2, 1884, "in
many ways occupies a place of its own among my
dramas; the method is in various respects a departure
from my earlier one." Ibsen was notoriously reticent
about his own works, and it is anybody's guess just what
these various respects are in which *The Wild Duck* is to
differ from his other plays. Even so, "the great silent
one" was astonishingly explicit about the tragicomic
tone that he wanted to prevail throughout the production of the play. Discussing the presentation of *The
Wild Duck* in the Copenhagen Royal Theater on April
3, 1898, he pointed out that there had been too much
farce in the production; that is, not only were there too

many "farcical effects" throughout the entire performance generally, but, more specifically, the actor playing
the role of Hjalmar Ekdal, Emil Poulsen, had presented
his part too satirically and farcically. "It is to be tragicomedy," Ibsen continued his criticism, "otherwise
Hedvig's death remains incomprehensible." [56]

What this means is not hard to gather: Hjalmar is evidently a comical figure—this Ibsen does not and could
not deny—but he apparently wants to indicate that one
is not merely to laugh at him but also to feel that sympathy for him which is usually reserved to the *dramatis
personae* of tragedy. Seen from this angle, the somewhat
cryptic assertion "otherwise Hedvig's death remains incomprehensible" implies that the shock and suffering
which the child's suicide brings upon the father should
be borne not by a shallow character drawn with the
merciless superiority of the satirist but by a character
created with sympathy and pity. Hence, Ibsen's insistence on "tragicomedy" as distinguished from satire,
farce, or comedy. This interpretation (which tends to
place Hjalmar in the center of the play) is borne out by
a letter Ibsen wrote to H. Schrøder, the manager of the
Kristiania theater, on November 14, 1884 concerning
the choice of an actor for the role of Hjalmar:

This part must definitely not be played with any kind of
parody of expression; there must be no trace that the actor is
conscious of there being any kind of comic element in the
lines at all. He has that endearing quality in his voice, says
Relling, and that must be maintained above all. His soulful-
ness is genuine, his moodiness beautiful in its way, not a trace
of affectation. In confidence, I might direct your attention to
Kristofer Jansen who can really be very nice when he is talking his worst drivel.

In other words: above and beyond the obvious ludicrous traits in Hjalmar's character, his more positive
features, his human worth and dignity, should be
brought out; that is to say, exactly those elements which
make the ludicrous figure the object of the audience's

pity and sympathy and make him a potentially tragic figure. On this point, most critics seem to be agreed. Even Hermann J. Weigand's reading of the play, guided as it is by the warning that "we must keep a close tether on our emotions," does not fail to perceive, for all its attention to the comic nuances of Hjalmar's theatricality, that there is an "undercurrent of sympathy" in the audience's attitude to this character.[57]

Still, it remains to be shown just how Ibsen achieved this integration of comic and tragic effects, especially in the main character, Hjalmar Ekdal, the dilettante photographer in the garret who fancies himself a genius of invention. Hjalmar, around whom all the characters and the action are rather neatly centered, is indeed the triumph of Ibsen's workmanship in this play. He has been duped into believing that all's right with his world, and from the outset the drama is concerned with the shattering of this illusion. This kind of motif is, of course, familiar in farce, but clearly Hjalmar is not the type of *dramatis persona* that farce usually requires as the butt of its derisive banter; rather, he is, in spite of all his ridiculousness, a person of human worth and substance which makes him not a comic but a tragicomic victim of the illusion and the shattering of the illusion which is imminent in four out of the five acts of the play. The final act shows the equally tragicomic re-birth of the inadequate relation to reality that had been Hjalmar's problem all along.

In the first act, which is largely and, it must be admitted, somewhat clumsily dedicated to the exposition—that is, to the revelation of the past which is then brought to bear on the present situation of the characters—we are made to anticipate the impending disaster that is to overtake Hjalmar. The scene is laid in the elegantly furnished house of Werle, the wholesale merchant and manufacturer who in the past was closely associated with the Ekdal family in a variety of ways, too closely for comfort in fact, as it soon emerges. A party

in honor of Werle's recently returned son, Gregers, is in
progress. Hjalmar Ekdal, Gregers' boyhood friend, is
present, and though he makes only a relatively brief appearance and even then by no means dominates the conversation, he is, dramatically speaking, the life of the
party since most of the conversation is directly or indi-
rectly concerned with him and his family and their past
in particular. And as this past is gradually revealed, at
first with hints, but progressively in a more straightfor-
ward manner, Hjalmar begins to be enshrouded by the
tragicomic atmosphere that will surround him until the
last moment of the play.

There are, more exactly, *two* circumstances in the
past of the Ekdal family that are revealed, one about
which Werle, Gregers, and Hjalmar are fairly well informed and one which only gradually comes to light
and of which neither Gregers nor Hjalmar had the
slightest inkling when the play opened. The first and
relatively harmless fact to come to light is that several
years before, Werle and Hjalmar's father were involved
in a crooked timber deal from which Werle emerged
with his reputation unscathed while old Ekdal was sent
to jail. Hjalmar has never quite gotten over this scandal
and his family's loss of bourgeois respectability. In the
framework of the mentality and value assumptions of
the world of *The Wild Duck*, this is the worst loss that
can possibly happen to a man (121, 157-158).* Thus, it is
quite understandable that Hjalmar speaks of this "catastrophe" in the most depressed and painful terms; and he
is entirely convincing in his expression of grief. But is
there not just a shade of comical exaggeration in the
whimpering way he expresses himself on the subject after
all these years: "(*In a gloomy tone*): But inwardly—
that's another story! I don't have to tell you all that I've

* All page references to *The Wild Duck* are from *The Wild
Duck and Other Plays*, tr. by Eva Le Gallienne, Modern Library,
New York: Random House, Inc. Copyright 1961 by Eva Le Gal-
lienne.

been through. You know all about *that* catastrophe!
. . . Don't speak of it! The poor, miserable old man! I
look after him, of course; he lives with me. He has no
one else to turn to. But it's too painful to talk about . . .
all that ghastly business" (108-109). A little later in the
act, this whining, self-pitying tone is accented even
more clearly (116), and as the action progresses this
tone will indeed become Hjalmar's hallmark.

There are intimations that Werle had his share of
guilt in the ruin of Hjalmar's father. But these are
quickly overshadowed by the allusions to old Werle's
even greater complicity in the other scandal that is
about to destroy whatever comfort, happiness, and respectability is left in Hjalmar's own life. It develops in
the conversation of the old school friends that after that
"catastrophe" Werle, though publicly shunning the
Ekdals, not only set up Hjalmar in his photography
business but also arranged his marriage to his, Werle's,
own former housekeeper. We already know, since the
opening of the play, in fact, that housekeepers in that
family have the amorous inclinations of the master of
the house to contend with. So one begins to wonder
why Werle should want to marry his housekeeper off to
young Ekdal and feather his bed the way he did. "It's
funny—one would almost think he was trying to atone
for something," says Gregers even before he has heard
that Mrs. Ekdal is the former Gina Hansen (110).
Hjalmar a cuckold before marriage perhaps? This
would make the "catastrophe" complete, and yet, just as
in the discussion of the business scandal, Ibsen makes
sure that the audience understands that it is a slightly
ridiculous character to whose happiness and respectability this threat is posed. In discussing his marital happiness, Hjalmar points with comical pride to the fact that
his wife is not entirely without education, adding
"Life's the best education, when you come right down
to it. And, being so much with me, she—And I've a
couple of very brilliant friends who drop in almost

every day" (111). Under Gregers' probing questioning
more and more suspicious factors come to light, and the
dramatist very skilfully maintains the comic-tragic ambiguity that they create. "So it worked out very neatly,
didn't it?" Gregers asks, and Hjalmar rises, pleased: "Yes
—wasn't it amazing? It really worked out very neatly"
(112). The point is, of course, that Gregers, suspecting
some foul play, is a trifle ironic while Hjalmar is dead
serious, not even guessing that Gregers suspects anything at all. This is no doubt one of the subtle, funny
highlights of the drama, but Hjalmar's very naïveté reminds us that we are also face to face with a potentially
tragic victim of a clever intrigue, which, if it should be
revealed, will ruin this slightly comic figure. At this
point he says about Werle: "He came to the rescue of
his old friend's son. That shows what a kind heart he
has!" (112). To add poignancy, Ibsen has him say this at
the very moment when Werle enters arm in arm with
his present housekeeper who promptly addresses him as
"dear Mr. Werle" (112) and, a little later on, shows
such a curiously discrete concern for Gina and the
Ekdal family (116).

We learn what sort of a heart Mr. Werle really
has in the subsequent argument between father and
son with which the first act concludes. In the course
of this heated discussion Gregers confirms his worst suspicions about the Hjalmar-Gina marriage. Werle,
Gregers intimates, was "extremely interested" in Gina
(119), and all he has done for old and young Ekdal
stems from a feeling of guilt, and Werle's squirming
seems to confirm the intimation. "Yes! And he's there
now—with that noble, trusting, childlike mind of his—
living under the same roof with that degraded creature
—quite unaware that what he calls his home is built on
nothing but a lie! . . . When I look back on all the
wicked things you've done, I feel as though I were gaz-
ing at some ghastly battlefield—strewn with shattered
corpses," (123) Gregers tells his father and leaves his

house for good. One need not accept every favorable adjective with which he endows his friend Hjalmar, but even so, young Ekdal, as he has so far been presented, has enough human worth and dignity to make him a potentially "tragic" hero so that the threat that from now on overshadows his existence may not easily be dissolved in the derisive laughter of farce (which, as we noted, Ibsen tried to curb). True, as we see the curtain fall on the first act, we *also* remember Hjalmar as the slightly comical sentimental phraseur. As such, he would tinge the grim light of the tragedy that is about to evolve with the hue of comedy.

In clever alternation with the dominant note with which the first act dismisses us, Hjalmar's *comic* features are emphasized the moment he appears in the second act. He returns home from the Werle party and immediately starts bragging to his family about the grand role he played there, which is, of course, purely imaginary. Posing as the connoisseur he will never be and as the bold social critic that he never was, he shows a good bit more amusing vanity than one would ordinarily expect from a tragic hero (130-131). Also, having previously appeared as enduring his multifarious family woes with renunciation and noblesse of mind, he now seems to be given to comical egotistical petulance when he says: "The head of the family is expected to think of everything—it's quite amazing! If by chance he forgets the slightest thing, he's immediately surrounded by glum faces. Well—one has to get used to it, I suppose" (132). Whereas Gregers called Hjalmar childlike, one wonders if childish would not have been the more suitable description of his attitude, of which he gives several samples as soon as he has returned home. He poses as the pouting little boy who thinks himself wronged ("No flute for me; no pleasures of any sort for *me.* . . . All I have to look forward to is *work*" [133]). Then again he is overcome by an equally childish sense of guilt about his having dined "at the rich man's table" while his poor miserable family waits for his return. All this, slightly theatrical as it is, has a comical effect, of course. The same may be said about Hjalmar's next melodramatic declamation: "Our rooms may be poor and humble, Gina—but they're home all the same. And I can say from the bottom of my heart: it's good to be here" (134). "Highly sentimental"—exactly like the tune he played on the flute just a moment before, and as such highly amusing. But if we recall at this point that this marital happiness, no matter how trashily expressed, is about to be destroyed, we sense that close at hand is a much severer "catastrophe" than the business scandal discussed in the first act ever was.

And, indeed, just at this moment who should appear but Gregers, whose very presence brings this threat to mind, and as if to show just how much is at stake, Ibsen carefully uses the first minutes of the ensuing conversation to portray the intimacy of this family in its joys as well as its sorrows. This is done by discussing Hjalmar's daughter, Hedvig, who—like Mr. Werle, senior—is losing her eyesight. But no sooner has the genuine togetherness of the Ekdal family been suggested than Gregers is allowed to ask more probing questions about the circumstances leading to Gina's and Hjalmar's marriage, and darker clouds gather over the proletarian idyll. "How long is it now since you were married?" (136). There is undoubtably a sense of impending doom as Gregers pursues this line of investigation. It becomes even more pointed as Gregers jumps at the opportunity to lodge with the Ekdals while Gina distinctly resents and opposes the idea (142-144). Naturally, Hjalmar would be the most severely struck by the shattering of the illusion on which his marriage seems to be built. This we can foresee even at this early point, especially since Ibsen has made it clear so far that his family life means everything to Hjalmar. But while the dramatist does not allow us to forget this, he concludes the second act with a few strokes in the character portrait of Hjalmar that make

us smile: "You really are amazing!" he says to Gina, "I
thought you were so hipped on renting it—and now
you behave as though you didn't want to. . . . Mr.
Werle [senior] has done a lot for me . . ." (144-145).
Not only does Hjalmar appear in the light of comedy at
this moment, but we also notice that what makes him
appear ridiculous is exactly the same thing that, even at
this point, creates, in our carefully nurtured anticipation, the aura of tragedy and impending doom about
him: namely, the illusion on which his family life is
based. As the act closes there is a hint of yet another
illusion under which Hjalmar is laboring: his slightly
megalomaniac notion that he was born to carry out an as
yet unspecified "sacred duty in life," an overpowering
task which he speaks about in such pompous terms that
we find it hard to take him seriously (145).

In the third act, Hjalmar's illusions are still not destroyed. The main function of this central part of the
play is, rather, to increase the audience's apprehension
that the disaster is about to overtake Hjalmar. Perhaps it
is significant that the one picture that Hedvig remem-
bers from Harrison's *History of London*, which she
speaks about in this act, is one "of death holding an
hourglass—and he has a lady with him" (152). That
particular variety of death, which must be worse than
physical death in the bourgeois society presented in *The
Wild Duck*, namely, the death of bourgeois respectability and the death of family happiness, is lurking in the
wings throughout this act. But as the clouds of impending doom gather about Hjalmar, Ibsen is again careful to
remind us of his protagonist's comical weaknesses, his
hollow and self-pitying theatricality, in particular. "I'll
carry on as long as my strength holds out," says the
photographer bored by his routine work and thinking
of the higher things that he believes he is born for—
though it is not only work on his invention that he longs
for but also diversion in the attic where his father has
built a dream world of the hunter *manqué*. "Never you

fear, Hedvig; while your father keeps his health—" and
off he sneaks into the attic (149). A genuinely funny
scene. But when Gregers' knock on the door puts a sudden end to the scene, it is just as full of disastrous fore-
boding as that other famous literary knock preceding
the porter scene in *Macbeth*. And this fearful anticipation is by no means disappointed: Gregers plunges into
another round of exploratory and suggestive questioning that keeps fresh in our memory the deadly threat to
Hjalmar's existence.

But before our fears come true, the conversation
shifts once again to that other illusion that gives Hjalmar security. The "sacred duty" which he spoke of at
the end of the previous act turns out to be his photographic invention which he apparently has been "work-
ing" on but which quite clearly is not to be taken seriously. Thus, once again, Hjalmar appears as the comic
fool, the fake, the dupe of his own grand schemes even
while the audience is already aware of the tragic calamity drawing closer and closer. Yet Ibsen very ingen-
iously leads our attention back to this impending disaster by driving home its gravity. We hear that by his
dubious invention (that he can as yet not say a thing
about) Hjalmar plans to give his father "back his self-
respect by restoring the name of Ekdal to its former
dignity and honor" (157)—a sly reminder of what
counts in the world of the Ekdals and the Werles and of
what is about to be destroyed the minute Gregers tells
Hjalmar of his past. When he does so, we sense that
once again the world will come to a "stand-still," that
life will once again be "under an eclipse"—just as it had
when old Ekdal's business scandal was made public
(158). And as we faintly realize this possibility again,
Gregers makes his first unmistakable move to reveal to
Hjalmar that his happiness is an "illness," which he is
about to cure by opening his eyes (160). Hjalmar's first
reaction to this attempt is distinctly tragicomic: "My
dear Gregers—please don't go on about illnesses and

poisons any more! I dislike that kind of talk. In my house no one ever speaks to me about unpleasant things" (160). It is his indirect relation to reality that makes Hjalmar comic and tragic at the same time: his love of illusion reaches ridiculous proportions at this point; it is the inadequacy of this attitude that we find funny, and this inadequacy is precisely what invites the impending disaster.

As if to sharpen our awareness of the extremely bitter nature of this calamity, the dramatist parallels for several minutes Gregers' attempts to open Hjalmar's eyes and Dr. Relling's endeavors to foil his design by accentuating the happiness that prevails in the Ekdal household (162-164). In a way, then, it is Hjalmar's fate that is at stake in this exchange of the two outsiders. Hjalmar himself is comparatively passive while it goes on, but what glimpses we get of him show him as the tragicomic dupe of his illusions. Hjalmar, of course, does not know of the illusion that Gregers is driving at and which Dr. Relling seems to know about; so Ibsen has him talk about that other illusion of his (which, of course, he does not see through either), namely his photographic invention. It is pathetic to hear him talk of the happiness his invention will bring to his poor daughter ("*Then* you'll see! Your future will be taken care of . . . ," 163), and yet it is supremely funny as we know that the father, lovingly concerned about his child, is merely speaking of the preposterous *illusion* of an invention. In the mind of the audience both of these illusions (Hjalmar's invention and his solidly founded happy family life) are related by association; one recalls the other, and vice versa, since they are only two expressions of Hjalmar's precarious relation to reality. At the end of the act the shattering of Hjalmar's illusions is close at hand: Gregers finally seems to be within grasping distance of success as he leaves with Hjalmar for a walk on which he will open his friend's eyes.

This is, indeed, what happens between the acts. When

Hjalmar returns home in the fourth act he echoes Gregers' talk about the claim of the ideal; and as though their roles had been exchanged, he now begins to question Gina about the circumstances preceding their marriage some fifteen years ago. The dramatic significance of this device is that, though the audience was not made a witness of the revelatory conversation between the two friends, it is not cheated out of the experience of the shattering of Hjalmar's life-long illusion that it has been anticipating all along. And a tragicomic experience it is. Admittedly, Hjalmar's expression of shock and grief is genuine to begin with: "(*Paces about*): So this is my Hedvig's mother! And to think that I owe all I possess—(*Kicks a chair*) my home and everything that's in it, to a man who was your former lover! To that damned scoundrel Werle!" (173). One cannot doubt the unadulterated sincerity of the distress of this husband and father who suddenly sees the foundations of his happiness crumbling under him. And yet it takes Hjalmar only a few minutes to let his characteristic theatricality creep into his lamentation, and that, of course, removes him from the confines of tragedy pure and simple to that borderland between the two major dramatic genres where twilight never fades or darkens. When Hjalmar is allowed to expostulate about his "ardent, sensitive nature" (174), we cock our ears for the ridiculous, and there it is, slightly tinged, of course, with the lasting effect of sadness which was accentuated just a moment ago: "I was happy here too; I loved my home. But it was all a delusion! How I shall ever find the necessary inspiration now to bring my invention to fruition, heaven knows! It will die with me, I expect. And it will be your fault—it will be your past, Gina, that will have killed it" (174-175). Clearly, the easy transition from one illusion to the other not only shows that they are both somehow related; it also places the comic aspect of Hjalmar's illusion and disillusionment into sharper focus.

This becomes even more obvious—so much so that one almost tends to forget that Hjalmar is *also* the tragic cuckold—as he goes on to say: "What's become of the poor breadwinner's dream now! As I lay in there on the sofa, incessantly brooding over my invention, I realized only too well that the effort of creation was fast sapping my strength. I had a premonition: I knew that day would be my last! I saw you in my dream—the proud widow of the inventor—sad, but prosperous and grateful" (175). The sentimentality of this tirade is so overt as to make it deliciously comic, and yet we believe Hjalmar when he says to Gregers a little while later that he had "just been through the bitterest moments" of his life (175). It is indeed the severest catastrophe imaginable in this world where respectability in a narrow sense of the word and idyllically bourgeois family happiness are the highest values, and it is, of course, these that are both destroyed at one stroke.

Still, the worst is yet to come. Ibsen carries the disillusionment one step further by suggesting (though not definitely asserting) that not only was Werle Gina's lover but that he is also Hedvig's father. And even at this turn of the screw the dramatist contrives to show the tragic-comic ambiguity of Hjalmar's situation. There is brief mention of Werle's going blind. Hjalmar says, "(*With a start*): Blind? He's going blind you say? That's very strange" (181). So is Hjalmar's behavior, especially in view of the fact that he has previously expressed unconcern and cool indifference about his benefactor. The thought of *Hedvig's* blindness must, of course, have been crossing his mind at this moment, and the audience reacts with awe in anticipation of still more shattering revelations about the Ekdal family's past which have been hinted at now and then. Gina behaves strangely, too, in her response to Hjalmar's shock about Werle's going blind ("Lots of people do, unfortunately," 181), and thus she does anything but allay our apprehension of still graver tragedy. But the threat of tragedy passes. As it does so, Hjalmar is again allowed to make a fool of himself so that the audience is led to realize that if Hjalmar should become the target of a yet severer disillusionment, he would also be a somewhat comic victim.

This reminder is just in time to preserve the tragicomic balance that characterizes the play, for when the tragic revelation finally does come with full force toward the end of the act, that is, when Hjalmar becomes convinced that he is not Hedvig's father, the ridiculousness of the dupe is all but obscured:

> HJALMAR: Answer me! Does Hedvig belong to me—or—? Well?
> GINA (*Looks at him coldly and defiantly*): I don't know.
> HJALMAR (*Trembling slightly*): You don't know?
> GINA: No. How should I? A creature like me—?
> HJALMAR (*Quietly turning away from her*): Then I have nothing more to do in this house (187).

It would be hard to contend that this is the theatrical poseur speaking. The simplicity of the language, reënforced by the simplicity of mimetic representation, is undoubtedly meant to show us Hjalmar's tragedy and nothing but his tragic suffering in his moment of truth. But Ibsen's aesthetic detachment is such that he manages to point to the element of comedy even in the bitterest moment of tragedy. When, in reply to Gregers' quick warning to consider what he is doing, Hjalmar exclaims: "What is there to consider? For a man like me there can be no alternative," we cannot resist the urge to smile since this statement of Hjalmar's is a clear reference to Hjalmar's newly acquired sense of the "claim of the ideal," and we already know that Hjalmar is not quite the person to live up to such high expectations. Thus, if we take the two bits of dialogue together, a shade of the comic is inevitably intermixed with the tragic even at the point of its most intense expression. The two are blended perfectly in each sentence and each word immediately after this exchange when Hjalmar leaves his house and family with an expression of tragic pathos, which has just enough sentimental exaggeration in it to suggest that while his suffering is tragic, he suffers comically: "I don't want to," he replies to Gregers' suggestion that he should take the chance to "start afresh in a spirit of forgiveness and self-sacrifice." "Never, Never! My hat! (*Takes his hat*) My home is nothing but a mass of ruins! (*Bursts into tears*) Gregers! I have no child!" (187). More drastic exaggeration of Hjalmar's theatricality would easily have been possible, but the subtle effect would have been destroyed by such extreme means; the caricature would have obscured the essential fact that we are dealing with a potentially tragic hero. Instead, Ibsen intended the tragic-comic *clair-obscure*, and in employing artistic restraint in order to achieve it, he once again proved himself the master of the nuance, which he has frequently been called.

In a way, this is the climax of the drama. It is hard to imagine how the tragicomic integration of effects could be carried any further and how new aspects of Hjalmar's illusion and disillusionment could be exploited for such tragicomic effects. Realizing this, Ibsen aptly introduces the last act of the play with a retrospective discussion of Hjalmar's case. To be sure, it is primarily a clinical anatomy of the advantages and disadvantages of the "Basic Lie . . . that makes life possible," in rather general terms at that, not only of Hjalmar's illusion which has just been destroyed. But as Gregers and Dr. Relling comment on Hjalmar's particular malaise and its questionable cure, Ibsen sees to it that the comic as well as the tragic is brought out. To achieve this double effect, he uses the point of view technique. That is to say, in Werle's comments, Hjalmar appears as the tragic hero who has his "spiritual crisis" and his "spiritual upheaval"; in Dr. Relling's comments as the comic fool whose ridiculousness stands revealed at last (192-195).

This would seem to be the last word on the matter: Hjalmar's dismissal papers, as it were, authoritatively stamped by Dr. Relling's professional approval and the traditionally creditable seal of the idealist. And yet, as Hjalmar himself enters the stage, the dramatist presents us with still another surprise, which, occurring in the second half of the last act, accentuates the tragicomic nature of the main character in yet another, quite novel way.

Now the tragicomic effects are no longer derived from the delusion of the protagonist and the gradual destruction of this delusion, for when Hjalmar appears in the last act, there is no longer any doubt in his mind as to the reality that he must face. He is eager and ready to honor the "claim of the ideal," with which Gregers has imbued him. Practically, this means that he is going to leave his family. And this is what he is getting ready for when he comes on stage. But it turns out that in the very preparations for life according to the ideal, Hjalmar is unable to live up to the ideal. Weak, comfort-loving, and half-hearted, he lacks the format of the traditional tragic protagonist who would have endured this crisis "heroically," living up to the dictates of his conscience, no matter how painful. Not so Hjalmar Ekdal. Instead of leaving his house, he again succumbs to its spell. To be sure, he only puts off his departure, but the audience is sure that he will never leave, and towards the end of the play, there is no more talk of his departure at all, nor will there ever be. His family life is definitely restored. What this means with regard to the theme of the drama is obvious: as soon as he has come out of his tragicomic delusion, Hjalmar plunges himself, whether intentionally or unintentionally we shall never know, into the same *self*-delusion, and this, of course, is equally tragicomic. Formerly he did not face reality because he did not know what it was; now he does not face reality because he knows it. In either case, he is duped: by reality before, by himself now. The aesthetic effect is the same. There is no need to point out the comedy of this restoration of Hjalmar's family life, of his return to his delusion by blinding himself to the facts of his life or to the attitude that he knows he should take to it. The comedy is, in fact, obvious to a fault. Yet the tragedy is nonetheless hinted at in no uncertain terms, for while Hjalmar now willingly adjusts himself to the delusion that his family life has been for him all along, he now for the first time acutely feels the mental anguish that is implied in it: Nothing is genuine for Hjalmar any more now that the myth of his family happiness has been exploded, not even the love of his daughter for him.

I loved her with all my heart—fool that I was! And I imagined that she loved me just as deeply in return. . . . I'm tormented by the thought that perhaps Hedvig never really cared for me at all. . . . Just think of all *they* have to offer her! And I who have loved her so deeply—! My greatest happiness would have been to take her hand and lead her through life, as one might lead a frightened child through a dark, empty room. But—I'm convinced of it now!—the poor photographer up in his garret has never meant anything to her at all. She was just being shrewd; trying to keep on the good side of him until something better came along (204-205).

The sudden crumbling of the foundations of his life have wrought havoc with Hjalmar's emotions, and surely Ibsen expects the audience to feel that kind of sympathy with him that it usually feels in great tragedy. Still, it is only one step from the tragic to the ludicrous, and under the impact of the force of Hjalmar's emotional outburst, we nearly forget that the dramatic craftsman takes that step here as he had done elsewhere in the play: Hjalmar's suspicions about the love of his daughter Hedvig are, as we well know by now, such an absurd misinterpretation of the reality that they do not fail to strike us also as slightly funny, its painfully sad implications for Hjalmar's state of mind notwithstanding. And just as throughout the drama, it is again Hjalmar's inadequate, delusive relation to reality that makes him comic and tragic at the same time.

The Wild Duck ends with a shock. A shot is heard
from the attic; Hedvig has killed herself. The motiva-
tion is not entirely satisfactory although psychologists,
forgetting that they are dealing with a play and not with
a case history, have been eloquent in their explanations.
What matters is how Hjalmar reacts to the suicide of his
daughter. "Oh, God! And I drove her from me like a
dog! She died for love of me: she crept into the attic,
filled with grief and terror, and died for love of me!
(*Sobs*) Never to be able to tell her! Never to be able to
atone! (*Clenches his fists and looks upwards shouting*)
You, up there—! If you *are* there—! Why have you
done this thing to me!" (209).

At this point, during the last minutes of the drama,
tragedy pure and simple seems to prevail irrevocably.
Needless to say, this would mean that the characteristic
tone of the play changes radically at the last moment.
But it does not, in fact. Even in the face of the most
gripping agony of his characters, Ibsen remained de-
tached, cleverly suggesting the comic overtones of the
tragedy. Was not Hjalmar's lamentation a trifle too de-
clamatory and, thus, not to be taken entirely seriously,
we wonder, remembering that Hjalmar is, after all, a
virtuoso of self-pitying rhetoric. And indeed, the dramatist wants us to nurture precisely this suspicion, for he
has Dr. Relling cast these doubts on Hjalmar's protesta-
tion of grief, doubts which, of course, make it appear a
little amusing for all the suffering they express.

Most people are noble in the presence of death. One wonders how long this nobility will last. . . . Before this year is
out, little Hedvig will be no more than a theme on which
to exercise his eloquence. . . . We'll talk of this again when
this year's grass has withered on her grave. You'll see: He'll
be spouting about "the child snatched from her father's
loving arms by an untimely death"; he'll be wallowing in a
sea of self-pity and maudlin sentimentality. You wait. You'll
see (210).

The dramatic intent and function of this remark is that the audience begins to "see" even now. And as the curtain falls, the spectators retain an image of Hjalmar Ekdal that is untainted by features distracting from the characteristic trait that Ibsen had been endeavoring to draw from the moment the protagonist appeared on the stage: a tragicomic dupe deceived by his world and, even more so, by himself.

The Philosophy of the Tragicomedian

At the outset of this chapter we proposed to discuss first the claim made by various writers and critics since the end of the eighteenth century that tragicomedy is the modern dramatic genre par excellence. This was to be followed by an analysis of the philosophical content it implies. It has, however, become clear by now that in practice a rigorous distinction of this kind is neither possible nor desirable. Our discussion of the many cases made for the modernity of the genre has inevitably involved an elucidation of the reasons given to make the cases plausible. If we had not proceeded in this fashion, our study would have degenerated into a mere listing of opinions expressed in favor of this particular dramatic genre. Such a listing would, however, be of only mild academic interest. Moreover, it would lay itself open to the charge that it was undertaken out of some merely terminological and classificatory interest. Such an interest may stem from an innate human need for establishing order among the phenomena of life and art; but it would still seem to be without any human significance, that is without significance as a contribution to our understanding of the human condition. It would, therefore, be in danger of becoming a purely academic game.

Such a procedure is always of dubious value, but it would be especially so in the case of tragicomedy. Every literary genre, the sonnet as well as the elegy, the heroic epic no less than satire, is essentially not a matter

of certain formal peculiarities and stylistic characteristics or of the subject treated but a matter of a specific
perception, a specific way of envisioning subject matter,
life, man, and the world. Every literary genre, therefore, shows us specific human possibilities of self-understanding. The investigation of literary genres is, as a result, in the last analysis a contribution to anthropology:
a contribution to our knowledge of man's understanding
of himself through the ages. If this is so, an investigation
of tragicomedy and its theory promises to be particularly rewarding, for it is in tragicomedy that the two
extremes that man is capable of in his self-evaluation are
united. Man is the only being that can laugh and weep.
Laughing and weeping can both be reactions to the
perception of the human condition *in extremis*. They
are, among many other things, the emotions aroused by
comedy and tragedy, respectively. Comedy and tragedy, however, confront man with the most extreme situations that he can experience. If, now, the comic and
the tragic visions are such distinctly human phenomena
and consequently of prime importance for our understanding of the nature of man, are we not justified in
assuming that the *union* of the two is likely to throw a
light on the human condition that promises to be particularly illuminating? Again, we have no intention of ele-
vating tragicomedy at the expense of other literary
genres which may seem to originate in a less comprehensive, less "total" vision of life and the world. We
simply ask: what does it mean for the image of man that
he is capable of viewing himself and his world as comic
and tragic at the same time? What precisely is the *Weltanschauung* implied in this double vision of the "tragedy and comedy of life"? [58] It has been called the highest,
the most satisfactory, and the most exhaustive statement
on the nature of man, but, as one might expect, usually
by its protagonists. [59] We shall try to be more specific.

We must begin with the realization that the "extraordinary *Weltanschauung*" that Heine imputed to tragi-

comedy allows a great many individual variations. The contents range from the highest "emotional fulfillment," namely "happiness," [60] to the most pessimistic despair.

Starting with the less disturbing interpretations of the tragicomic *Weltanschauung*, we might recall Kierkegaard's Frater Taciturnus in *Stages on Life's Way* who, analyzing the tragicomedy of Quidam-Kierkegaard's unhappy love, comments "I sit at my ease, cheerfully employed with my calculations, and look out over the tragic and the comic." [61] Even in Ionesco, in his play *Victims of Duty*, we find that a character remarks, in a curious formulation of the author's own pet theories, that "in harmony with the general drift of the other manifestations of the modern spirit" tragicomedy would be the genre of the future, for "the tragic's turning comic, the comic is tragic, and life's getting more cheerful." [62]

But what is the cause of this cheerfulness? One answer that suggests itself is that the ability to visualize the same object from two diametrically opposed points of view promotes a certain tolerance of things as they are: Since there is more than one way of looking at things, one's impatience with them might conceivably be modified and not necessarily with a frivolous shrug of the shoulders. Jean Paul, the German Romanticist, for instance, tended to such an all-encompassing understanding and sympathy in his theory of the identity of the comic and the tragic in his *Vorschule der Ästhetik* (*Introduction to Aesthetics*, 1804). J. L. Styan has recently revived this idea, claiming that a sense for the tragicomic in life helps us develop "a relevant philosophy of tolerance" and that therefore tragicomic drama should not be considered as "unhealthy" but as implicitly "didactic." [63] Christopher Fry's speculation on the comedy that arises out of tragedy points in a similar direction. For him, the final assertion of the comic spirit over the basic tragedy of existence spells affirmation of life and that joy that arises out of the depth of suffering.[64] This in turn can even be coupled with a feeling of ultimate metaphysical security as in the case of Jean Paul.

But such a firm attitude of assurance is by no means the only one that suggests itself even among the more comforting philosophies of the tragicomic. The laughter at the tragic quality of life, even in its profoundest aspect, can be a gesture of escape and the temporary alleviation that is associated with such an escape. This is a view which Ionesco, much like the mysterious Bonaventura, author of the *Night Watches*, has expressed with particular emphasis. For Ionesco, laughter is "the only opportunity we have of detaching ourselves from our tragi-comic human condition or the sickness of living. . . . To become fully conscious of the atrocious and to laugh at it is to master the atrocious." [65]

However, it is easy to see that the "outlet," the "release," the "salvation" [66] provided by the perception of the ridiculous aspect of a deeply tragic and painful situation can only be a temporary one. Sooner rather than later, it will give way to an awareness of the unrelieved pain that was felt to begin with.

It is such disillusionments that will then frequently lead not to an awareness of total tragedy but rather of total tragicomedy. Thus, Friedrich Schlegel, Schopenhauer, and other Romanticists can speak of "the tragicomedy of mankind." In Romanticism this is almost a *topos*, and in the everyday conversation of our time it has all but become a cliché and, thereby, trivial.

The notion does, however, become more interesting if it is applied to the metaphysical dimension. It was above all Kierkegaard who saw this. He associated an awareness of the tragicomic quality of life with "religion." "Religious seriousness," he said in *Stages on Life's Way*, "is, like religion itself, the higher passion which issues from the unity of the comic and the tragic." In another place in the same book he does, to be sure, specify that this "religiousness" results only from the *abstraction* of the tragic from this *unity*, whilst "to see at once the comic and the tragic in the same thing is the culmination of paganism." Even so, a relationship between the perception of the tragicomic and theology is clearly indicated, albeit "pagan" theology. And, indeed, it is a strangely pagan religiosity that we are dealing with. Thus, Kierkegaard has his Frater Taciturnus say in the same work that he is viewing the "unity of the comic and the tragic in a thoroughly Greek way. I imagine the blissful gods creating such a man for the sake of enjoying a dialectic pleasure in observing him." [67]

That is to say: once life and the world as a whole are considered to be an enormous tragic farce, "transcendental buffoonery" (Friedrich Schlegel),[68] the idea suggests itself that this tragicomedy might be presided over by some god for whose amusement the show, a puppet show usually, is carried on. The world appears as a "caprice of God" (Brentano)[69] and man as a marionette in a tragic farce of cosmic proportions—a tragic farce that appears painful to him and amusing to the god that directs it. This god might well be the "savage God" that Yeats spoke about after that memorable first performance of Jarry's *Ubu roi* (1896), naming him the patron of all future literature. It may be an overstatement that "the comedy of the savage god" is the catchphrase of all modern avant-garde drama, as it has been suggested, but undeniably there is, within the mainstream of modern drama, that distinct group of plays that Rosette Lamont has called the metaphysical farce: farce for the cruel gods, tragedy for man who is the victim of this divine sport. Actually, it was Romanticism that conceived of this frightening idea of comedy. But it failed to produce it. So did Strindberg who talks about it repeatedly in his *Inferno*, e.g., when he jots down "Perhaps in the depth of our souls there lurks a shadowy consciousness that everything down here is all humbug, a masquerade, a mere pretence, and that all our sufferings afford mirth to the gods" or again: "Ah! what a game the gods play with us poor mortals! And, therefore, in the most tormented moments of life, we too can laugh with self-conscious raillery." And finally, at the conclusion of this autobiographic work: "And then? After that? A new joke for the gods, who laugh heartily when we shed bitter tears." [70] One of the leading tragicomedians of our century, Pirandello, voices a similar conviction: "I believe that life is a very sad farce"; it is a farce because we constantly live in a world of illusion which is often cruelly shattered by realities. Once this game of ours is seen through, though, life loses all its attraction for us. Pirandello is one of those who feel this loss, but he turns his loss to advantage. He continues, "My art is full of bitter pity for all those who deceive themselves; but this pity must be followed by a grim laughter at fate which condemns man to this deception." [71]

Again, the conclusion that suggests itself most naturally in this context is that tragicomedy predicated on this kind of theological assumption is a *nihilistic* genre. But this may be a conclusion that can be reached only by a jump. For one thing, one would do well to recall Morgenstern's maxim that the consistent pessimist would "fall silent and—die," that is, would no longer write any more. The tone and the thought content of a given work of art may be nihilistic, and programmatically so, but the very act of writing negates this putative nihilism to a considerable extent. That is, it deprives it of its apodictic, assertive character; it turns a seeming statement into an actual *question*. Thus, even those tragicomedies that are most extreme in their pessimism and nihilism are not so much a result of nihilistic persuasion as of *skepticism*, a deeply troubled skepticism perhaps, but one which still asks questions and thus lives up to its genuine function. Even the direst nihilism, if expressed in words, let alone in a work of art, is not a statement but a provocation, for, obviously, the "nihilistic" writer does not find it meaningless and senseless to engage in the act of literary creation; and he finds it worthwhile to submit his own nihilism, such as it is, to his readers, in the secret hope, no doubt, of being refuted or at least of being confronted with questions. "Nihilistic" tragicomedy is, then, the challenge of a deeply concerned and wondering mind to his own age and, perhaps, to other ages as well.

Thus, tragicomedy of the extreme kind, that is the tragicomedy that is not informed by the didactic spirit that J. L. Styan attributes to it, is lacking in a positive note or a concrete ideological message. Ionesco, one of the most outspoken exponents of tragicomedy, was confronted with this charge by Kenneth Tynan, the British critic. He denied that it was a valid criticism. For "messages" have a curious way of boomeranging. Wars have been fought in order to improve the lot of mankind, Ionesco replies to his English critic's accusation. And he concludes with this profoundly humane paradox: "Do not improve the lot of mankind, if you really wish it well." [72] The tragicomedian is aware, if painfully so, that while "answers" are comforting and sometimes easy to provide, they tend to have a false ring. He would agree with a character in Audiberti's Pucelle* who points out that "it isn't the world's business to furnish us answers, but enigmas." [73] But to enigmas one can put questions, and *questions*, according to a maxim of Ibsen, Gertrude Stein, Max Frisch and others, are frequently more important than answers. Asking questions is in essence what the tragicomedian attempts to do in our time. He is—knowingly or unknowingly—far from asserting that "meaninglessness" is the last word. He does know, however, that he cannot "save the world." That is his wisdom and his despair—which drives him on to literary creation. "And thus we should not try to save the world," Dürrenmatt, who considers tragicomedy the only dramatic form suited to our time, remarks in one of his stories, "but to bear it. That is the one real

* © Editions Gallimard. By permission.

adventure which remains possible for us in this late time." [74] Tragicomedy is the literary genre, or one of the literary genres that embark on this adventure of the moderns. Later historians will see where it took us, and why.

NOTES
BIBLIOGRAPHY
INDICES

1. 223 c-d. *The Dialogues of Plato*, tr. by B. Jowett, 4th ed., I, Oxford: Clarendon Press, 1953, 555.
2. Tr. by Paul Nixon, *The Loeb Classical Library*, *Plautus*, I, London: Heinemann, 1916, 9, 11.
3. Cicero, *De Inventione, De Optimo Genere Oratorum, Topica, The Loeb Classical Library*, London: Heinemann, 1949, p. 354.
4. *The London Mercury*, IV, 31.
5. Barrett H. Clark, ed., *European Theories of the Drama*, New York: Crown Publishers, 1947, pp. 30-31.
6. Allan H. Gilbert, *Literary Criticism, Plato to Dryden*, New York: American Book Co., 1940, pp. 524-525.
7. *Tragicomedy: Its Origin and Development in Italy, France, and England*, 1955, p. 55.
8. Herrick, pp. 28-29.
9. G. Gregory Smith, ed., *Elizabethan Critical Essays*, I, New York: Oxford University Press, 1937, 199.
10. On Pontanus and Donatus see Nikolaus Nessler, "Die Dramaturgie der Jesuiten Pontanus, Donatus und Masenius," Programm Brixen: Vinzentinum, 1905, p. 23.
11. *Deutsche Literatur in Entwicklungsreihen, Reihe Barock, Barockdrama*, II, Leipzig, 1930, 38. In German, this meaning of comitragedy seems to have outlasted the seventeenth century; see Lichtenberg's letter to Kaltenhofer, August 23, 1773, in *Lichtenbergs Briefe*, Albert Leitzmann, ed., I, Leipzig: Dieterich, 1901, 163.
12. Baltimore: Furst, 1907, p. 36.
13. Note 9 above.
14. Herrick shows this in his Chapters 7 and 8.
15. Cf., Herrick, p. 260.
16. *Il Verato Secondo*, see Gilbert (note 6 above), p. 511.
17. Herrick, p. 319.
18. Ninth ed., II, 1814, 354. On similar views see C. C. Green, *The Neoclassic Theory of Tragedy in England*, Harvard, 1934, pp. 168 f.

19. Translated from Lessing's translation from the French
    into German (Lessing, *Sämmtliche Werke*, eds. Lach-
    mann and Muncker, VI, 16.).

20. *Kants Kritik der Urteilskraft*, I, Halle, 1923.

21. König's edition of the *Gedichte* of Canitz, Leipzig and
    Berlin: Hauden, 1727, p. 256.

22. *Critische Beiträge*, VIII, 1742, 143-144.

23. *Philosophical Letters*, tr. by Ernest Dilworth, *The Li-
    brary of Liberal Arts*, Indianapolis: Bobbs Merrill, 1961,
    p. 89 (my text is slightly changed).

24. *J. E. Schlegels ästhetische und dramaturgische Schriften*,
    Joh. v. Antoniewicz, ed., *Deutsche Literatur-Denkmäler
    des 18. und 19. Jahrhunderts*, XXVI, Heilbronn, 1887,
    95. See note 30 below.

25. Wieland, *Werke*, Berlin: Hempel, n.d., XXXVI, 280.

26. Pierre Martino, ed., Paris, 1927, pp. 142-157.

27. Diderot, *Oeuvres Complètes*, J. Asselzat, ed., VII, Paris,
    1875, 137.

28. *Einleitung in die Schönen Wissenschaften*, 4th ed., II,
    Leipzig, 1774, 394.

29. See especially his commentary on *Henry IV*, Part two,
    I, iv.

30. Schlegel (note 24 above), 92-93. Nicolai in *Lessings
    Briefwechsel mit Mendelssohn und Nicolai über das
    Trauerspiel*, Robert Petsch, ed., *Philosophische Biblio-
    thek*, CXXI, Leipzig, 1910, 25-26.

31. *Works*, II, London, 1811, 84.

32. *Essays of John Dryden*, W. P. Ker, ed., I, Oxford: Clar-
    endon Press, 1900, 146-147.

33. *Oeuvres complètes*, IV, Paris, 1820, 287.

34. II, Barcelona: Selecciones Bibliófilas, 1956, 136-137 (Third
    part, Chapter 16).

35. *Opere*, M. Barbi and F. Ghisalberti, eds., II, Milano,
    1943, 332.

36. Clark (note 5 above), p. 189.

37. *Ibid*.

38. *Ibid.*, p. 122.

39. Book XII, Chapter 1. Quoted from Lessing, *Hambur-
    gische Dramaturgie*, Section LXIX. The text of the orig-
    inal version (1766-67) was not available to me in any
    other form.

40. See Karl S. Guthke, "Christian Weises Masaniello und
    die dramatische Tradition," *Revue des Langues Vivantes*,

XXV (1959), 402-410; and Guthke, *Geschichte und Poetik der deutschen Tragikomödie*, Göttingen: Vandenhoeck und Ruprecht, 1961, pp. 207-217, 226-248.

41. Note 24 above, 213.

42. *Hamburg Dramaturgy*, with a new introduction by Victor Lange, New York: Dover Publications, 1962, p. 172.

NOTES TO CHAPTER II

1. Eugène Ionesco, *Notes and Counter-Notes: Writings on the Theatre*, tr. by Donald Watson, New York: Grove Press, 1964, p. 27. Similarly: Kierkegaard, *Stages on Life's Way*, Princeton University Press, 1945, p. 381; Lukacs, *Archiv f. Soz.wiss.*, 1914, p. 683.

2. Ronald Peacock, *The Art of Drama*, London: Routledge and Kegan Paul, 1957, p. 189.

3. Compare J. L. Styan's remark (*The Dark Comedy*, Cambridge University Press, 1962, p. 242) that the "mixing" of empathy and distance is "the common ambivalence of all drama except extreme kinds of impersonal farces like that of the commedia dell' arte." See also E. A. Wright, *A Primer for Playgoers*, Englewood Cliffs: Prentice-Hall, 1958, pp. 21-26.

4. Friedrich Schiller, *Sämtliche Werke*, XII, Säkularausgabe, 198 ("Über Naive und Sentimentalische Dichtung").

5. Clark (see Chapter I, note 5), p. 393.

6. *Ibid.*, p. 395.

7. Ionesco (note 1 above), p. 233.

8. *Doctor Faustus*, tr. by H. T. Lowe-Porter, New York: Knopf, 1948, p. 304.

9. Note 1 above.

10. Cyrus Hoy, "Comedy, Tragedy, and Tragicomedy," *Virginia Quarterly Review*, XXXVI (1960), 110. Hoy's views are fully demonstrated in his book *The Hyacinth Room*, New York: Knopf, 1964. Compare Ronald Peacock, *The Poet in the Theatre*, New York: Harcourt, Brace, 1946, p. 153: both tragedy and comedy "spring from the tension between our imperfect life and our ideal aspirations."

11. Stanley G. Eskin, "*Tristram Shandy* and *Oedipus Rex:* Reflections on Comedy and Tragedy," *College English*, XXIV (1963), 273, 275.

12. Tr. by David F. Swenson, Princeton University Press, 1941, pp. 459, 462-464.

13. Note 1 above.

14. Eskin (note 11 above), 276.

15. Friedrich Georg Jünger, *Über das Komische*, 3rd ed., Frankfurt: Klostermann, 1948, p. 23.

16. G. Wilson Knight, *The Wheel of Fire*, 4th ed., London: Methuen, 1949, p. 160.

17. Clark (see Chapter I, note 5), p. 398.

18. *Poetische Werke*, X, Berlin: de Gruyter, 1961, 75.

19. Eduard Hartl, *Das Drama des Mittelalters*, in *Deutsche Literatur in Entwicklungsreihen, Reihe: Drama des Mittelalters*, I, Leipzig, 1937, 75.

20. Calvin King Quayle, "Humor in Tragedy," unpublished doctoral dissertation, University of Minnesota, 1958, p. 262.

21. *Works of Frederick Schiller*, IV, London: Bohn, 1849, 70.

22. Ionesco: (note 1 above), p. 144. Nietzsche: *Der Wille zur Macht*, No. 990, Musarion edition XIX, 332. Pirandello: see Domenico Vittorini, *The Drama of Luigi Pirandello*, Philadelphia: University of Pennsylvania Press, 1935, p. 89.

23. *Weavers:* Martin Greiner, *Zwischen Biedermeier und Bourgeoisie*, Göttingen 1952, pp. 47 f. Eliot: *Selected Essays*, New York: Harcourt, Brace, 1932, p. 104.

24. Sarcey: Clark (see Chapter I, note 5), p. 399. Odoyevsky's letter: see B. V. Varneke, *History of the Russian Theatre*, New York: Macmillan, 1951, p. 321. Lewis: L. M. and M. B. Price, *The Publication of English Literature in Germany*, Berkeley: University of California Press, 1934, p. 143.

25. Thompson, *The Anatomy of Drama*, Berkeley: University of California Press, 1946, p. 86. John Northam, *Ibsen's Dramatic Method*, London: Faber, 1953, p. 11.

26. Ionesco (note 1 above), p. 83.

27. Styan (note 3 above), p. 44. Brecht: see Lionel Abel, *Metatheatre*, New York: Hill and Wang, 1963, p. 97. Ionesco (note 1 above), pp. 209, 207.

28. *Shakespeare heute*, München: Langen-Müller, 1964, pp. 287 f.
29. See R. Grimm in *Sinn oder Unsinn*, Basel: Basilius Presse, 1962, p. 49.
30. Guthke, *Geschichte und Poetik der deutschen Tragikomödie*, p. 392. J. Stolnitz: *Philosophy and Phenomenological Research*, XVI (1955), 45-47. Knight: *The Wheel of Fire* (note 16 above), pp. 160 ff. J. Loewenberg, *Dialogues from Delphi*, Berkeley: University of California Press, 1949, pp. 1 ff.
31. New York: Doubleday, Doran, 1940, p. 250.
32. *The London Mercury*, IV (1921), 32-33.
33. Ionesco (note 1 above), p. 164.
34. *Hudson Review*, X (1957), 39 f.
35. Viktor Klemperer, "Komik und Tragikomik bei Molière," *Die Neueren Sprachen*, XXX (1922), 327 ff; see also Hanna Corbach in *Reallexikon der deutschen Literaturgeschichte*, IV, 93.
36. See N. W. Bawcutt's edition, London: Methuen, 1958. The play has no subtitle.
37. Robert Petsch, *Einführung in Goethes Faust*, 3rd ed., Hamburg, 1949, p. 27.
38. Clark (see Chapter I, note 5), pp. 372, 375.
39. Cambridge University Press, 1960, p. 254.
40. *Ibid.*
41. *Ibid.*, p. 255.
42. Karl Vietor, "Die Geschichte literarischer Gattungen," *Geist und Form*, Berne: A. Francke, 1952, p. 306.
43. *Ibid.*, p. 302.

NOTES TO CHAPTER III

1. Quoted from Pirandello, *Opere*, VI, Milano: Mondadori, 1960, 36.
2. "Tragedy and the Common Man," in: H. O. Waite and B. P. Atkinson, eds., *Literature for Our Time*, New York: Holt, 1953, pp. 196-199. See also Walter Jens, "Antikes und modernes Drama," *Jahresring*, 1960/61, 66-85; Dürrenmatt's *Theaterprobleme* (to be discussed later

in this chapter), John Gassner, "Forms of Modern Drama," *Comparative Literature*, VII (1955), 132, and Joseph Wood Krutch, "The Tragic Fallacy" in his book *The Modern Temper*, New York: Harcourt Brace, 1929.

3. *Avant-Garde: The Experimental Theater in France*, Berkeley: University of California Press, 1962, p. 205.

4. "The Comedy of Thornton Wilder," in *Modern Drama: Essays in Modern Criticism*, Travis Bogard and William J. Oliver, eds., New York: Oxford University Press, 1965, p. 371.

5. Cf., John Gassner, *Comparative Literature*, 1955, p. 132: "The same deflationary sensibility which weakened tragic art favored the development of other, intermediate, forms of drama. We may observe this development in a modern sort of tragicomedy or 'dark' comedy, with as wide a range as that spanned by *Uncle Vanya* and *Juno and the Paycock*."

6. *Stufen*, München, 1918, p. 56.

7. Adolf D. Klarmann, "Friedrich Dürrenmatt and the Tragic Sense of Comedy," *Tulane Drama Review*, IV (1960), No. 4, 77.

8. See Chapter II, note 1, pp. 19, 222. See also Ellen Douglas Leyburn, "Comedy and Tragedy Transposed," *The Yale Review*, LIII (1964), 553-562.

9. Jacques Guicharnaud, *Modern French Theatre from Giraudoux to Beckett*, New Haven: Yale University Press, 1961, p. 88.

10. *Ibid.*, p. 120.

11. *Autobiography*, New York: Macmillan, 1953, p. 210.

12. *The Theater of Protest and Paradox: Developments in the Avant-Garde Drama*, New York University Press, 1964, p. 16.

13. Note 3 above.

14. Ruby Cohn, *Yale French Studies*, XXIII (1959), 16. Rosette C. Lamont, *The French Review*, XXXII (1959), 319-328. J. S. Doubrovsky, *Yale French Studies*, XXIII (1959), 3-10.

15. *Sämtliche Werke*, V, Stuttgart und Augsburg, 1859, 718.

16. *Die Serapionsbrüder*, Part I, Section 1.

17. Friedrich Schlegel, *Prosaische Jugendschriften*, 2nd ed., I, Jacob Minor, ed., Vienna, 1906, 107.

18. Note 15 above, 720-730. Similarly, Mundt, *Ästhetik*, 1845, pp. 340 f.

19. See *Über das Studium der griechischen Poesie*, 1797.
20. Weimar edition of the works, Part I, XLV, 177.
21. See Chapter I, note 5, p. 372.
22. *Ibid.* p. 374.
23. *The London Mercury*, IV (1921), 32 f.
24. *Ibsen*, tr. and ed. by James W. McFarlane, VI, New York: Oxford University Press, 1960, 440. Original in *Hundreårsutgave*, X, Oslo, 1932, 38.
25. *Our Theatres in the Nineties*, III, London: Constable, 1954, 138.
26. A. E. Zucker, *Ibsen, The Master Builder*, New York: Holt, 1929, p. 191.
27. Quoted from Wolfgang Kayser, *Die Wahrheit der Dichter*, Hamburg: Rowohlt, 1959, p. 130.
28. Guthke (see Chapter II, note 30), pp. 267-276.
29. *Three Tragedies of García Lorca*, New York: New Directions, 1947, p. 16.
30. *Seven Plays*, tr. and ed. by George Hauger, I, New York: Hill and Wang, 1960, 22.
31. *Luigi Pirandello*, London and Toronto: J. M. Dent, 1926, p. 41.
32. *Ibid.*, pp. 37-39.
33. Note 3 above, p. 204.
34. *Das Tragische als Weltgefühl und der Humor als ästhetische Gestalt des Metaphysischen*, Leipzig: Barth, 1931, p. 119. First published in 1877.
35. *L'Hurluberlu*, Paris: La Table Ronde, 1959, p. 112.
36. Hofmannsthal, *Prosa*, IV, Frankfurt: S. Fischer, 1955, 40.
37. Karl Holl, *Geschichte des deutschen Lustspiels*, Leipzig: Weber, 1923, pp. 343 f. Virgil Geddes, *Beyond Tragedy*, Seattle: University of Washington Book Store, 1930, pp. 15-17.
38. *Nachlese*, Berlin and Frankfurt: S. Fischer, pp. 29 ff.
39. Quoted from the reprint in *The Tulane Drama Review*, IV (1960), 77.
40. "Erlanger Rede über das absurde Theater," *Akzente*, VII (1960), 547, 551.
41. As quoted by Martin Esslin, *The Theater of the Absurd*, New York: Doubleday, 1961, p. 205.
42. See Chapter II, note 1, p. 213.
43. Elisabeth Brock-Sulzer, *Akzente*, III (1956), 47. Gerhard Nellhaus' translation of *Theaterprobleme* in *The Tulane Drama Review*, III, No. 1 (1958), 3-26, and in

Toby Cole's anthology *Playwrights on Playwriting*, New York: Hill and Wang, 1960, pp. 130-139, is lacking in accuracy.

44. Note 9 above, pp. 159 f.

45. *Essays*, New York, 1924, p. 297. Italics mine.

46. David Magarshack, *Chekhov the Dramatist*, New York: Auvergne, 1952, p. 273.

47. Raymond Alden, *Texas Review*, II (1916/17), 105.

48. Note 9 above, pp. 159 f.

49. *Das Groteske: Seine Gestaltung in Malerei und Dichtung*, Oldenburg: G. Stalling, 1957, p. 146.

50. Note 9 above, p. 162.

51. Rosette Lamont, "Death and Tragi-Comedy: Three Plays of the New Theatre," *Massachusetts Review* (Winter-Spring, 1965), 385.

52. McFarlane (note 24 above), 9.

53. All quotations from Ibsen's letters are from the appendix of McFarlane's volume, VI, 439-440.

54. All quotations from early comments on the play are from the appendix of McFarlane's volume, VI, 441-442.

55. For the context of Shaw's pronouncements on *The Wild Duck* see notes 23 and 25 above.

56. The wording of the 1898 interview was taken from the Ibsen Centennial Edition (*Hundreårsutgave*), X, Oslo 1932, 38.

57. *The Modern Ibsen*, New York: E. P. Dutton, 1960, pp. 146, 158.

58. Plato, *Philebos*, 50 b.

59. Johannes Volkelt, *System der Ästhetik*, II, München, 1910, 561.

60. Geddes (note 37 above), p. 17.

61. *Stages on Life's Way*, tr. by Walter Lowrie, Princeton University Press, 1945, p. 405.

62. *Plays*, II, London: Calder, 1958, 309.

63. Styan (See Chapter II, note 3), p. 292.

64. Note 39 above, 77 f.

65. See Chapter II, note 1, pp. 143 f.

66. *Ibid.*, p. 164.

67. Note 61 above, pp. 399, 383, 406.

68. *Lyceum*, Fragment No. 42.

69. *Godwi* in *Gesammelte Werke*, H. Amelung and K. Vietor, eds., II, 1923, 32.

70. Tr. by Claud Field, London: W. Rider, 1912, pp. 158, 176, 186.
71. *Opere* (note 1 above), VI, 1246.
72. See Chapter II, note 1, p. 106.
73. *Théâtre*, II, Paris: Gallimard, 1952, 173. (Translation from Pronko [note 3 above], p. 185).
74. *Der Verdacht*, Zürich: Arche, 1953, p. 155.

BIBLIOGRAPHY

ABEL, LIONEL. *Metatheatre: A New View of Dramatic Form*, New York: Hill and Wang, 1963.

BAHNSEN, JULIUS. *Das Tragische und der Humor*, Leipzig: J. A. Barth, 1931.

BENTLEY, ERIC. *The Life of the Drama*, New York: Atheneum, 1964.

CLARK, BARRETT H. *European Theories of Drama*, New York: Crown Publishers, 1947.

COHN, RUBY. "The Comedy of Samuel Beckett: 'Something Old, Something New,'" *Yale French Studies*, XXIII (1959), 11-17.

COLE, TOBY, ed. *Playwrights on Playwriting*, New York: Hill and Wang, 1960.

DORAN, MADELEINE. *Endeavors of Art: A Study of Form in Elizabethan Drama*, Madison: University of Wisconsin Press, 1954.

DOUBROVSKY, J. S. "Ionesco and the Comic of Absurdity," *Yale French Review*, XXIII (1959), 3-10.

DÜRRENMATT, FRIEDRICH. *Theaterprobleme*, Zürich: Arche, 1955. Tr. by Gerhard Nellhaus in *The Tulane Drama Review*, III, No. 1 (1958), 3-26.

EHRENPREIS, IRVIN. *The 'Types' Approach to Literature*, New York: King's Crown Press, 1945.

ESKIN, STANLEY G. "*Tristram Shandy* and *Oedipus Rex*: Reflections on Comedy and Tragedy," *College English*, XXIV (1963), 271-277.

ESSLIN, MARTIN. *The Theatre of the Absurd*, Anchor Books, Garden City, N. Y.: Doubleday, 1961.

FAUCONNIER, R. L. "Tragedy and the Modern Theatre," *Queen's Quarterly*, LV (1948), 327-332.

GASSNER, JOHN. "Forms of Modern Drama," *Comparative Literature*, VII (1955), 129-143.

GEDDES, VIRGIL. *Beyond Tragedy*, Seattle: University of Washington Book Store, 1930.

GRIMM, REINHOLD. "Das italienische Teatro grottesco," in

Sinn oder Unsinn? Das Groteske im modernen Drama,
by Martin Esslin *et al., Theater unserer Zeit,* III, Basel
and Stuttgart: Basilius Presse, 1962, 47-94.

GUICHARNAUD, JACQUES. *Modern French Theatre from Giraudoux to Beckett,* New Haven: Yale University Press,
1961.

GUTHKE, KARL S. *Geschichte und Poetik der deutschen
Tragikomödie,* Göttingen: Vandenhoeck und Ruprecht,
1961.

———. "Das Problem der gemischten Dramengattung in
der deutschen Poetik und Praxis vom Mittelalter bis zum
Barock," *Zeitschrift für deutsche Philologie,* LXXX
(1961), 339-364.

———. "Die Auseinandersetzung um das Tragikomische
und die Tragikomödie in der Ästhetik der deutschen
Aufklärung," *Jahrbuch für Ästhetik und allgemeine
Kunstwissenschaft,* VI (1961), 114-138.

HATCHER, ANNA GRANVILLE. *Modern English Word-For-
mation and the Neo-Latin,* Baltimore: Johns Hopkins
University Press, 1951.

HEILMAN, ROBERT B. "Tragedy and Melodrama; Speculations on Generic Form," *Texas Quarterly,* III (1960), No.
2, 36-50.

HERRICK, MARVIN T. *Tragicomedy: Its Origin and Devel-
opment in Italy, France, and England, Illinois Studies in
Language and Literature,* XXXIX, Urbana: University of
Illinois Press, 1955. Reprinted as Vol. IV of *Illini Books,*
Urbana: University of Illinois Press, 1962.

HILDESHEIMER, WOLFGANG. "Erlanger Rede über das absurde Theater," *Akzente,* VII (1960), 543-556.

HOCKE, GUSTAV RENÉ. *Manierismus in der Literatur,* Hamburg: Rowohlt, 1959.

HOY, CYRUS. "Comedy, Tragedy, and Tragicomedy," *Virginia Quarterly Review,* XXXVI (1960), 105-118.

———. *The Hyacinth Room: An Investigation into the
Nature of Comedy, Tragedy, and Tragicomedy,* New
York: Knopf, 1964.

IONESCO, EUGÈNE. *Notes and Counter Notes: Writings on
the Theatre,* New York: Grove Press, 1964.

JANENTZKI, CHRISTIAN. "Über Tragik, Komik und Humor,"
Jahrbuch des Freien Deutschen Hochstifts, 1936-1940, pp.
3 ff.

KAYSER, WOLFGANG. *Das Grosteske: Seine Gestaltung in*

Malerei und Dichtung, Oldenburg: G. Stalling, 1957.
Also English translation: *The Grotesque in Art and Literature,* tr. by U. Weisstein, Bloomington: Indiana University Press, 1963.

KLARMANN, ADOLF D. "Dürrenmatt and the Tragic Sense of Comedy," *Tulane Drama Review,* IV (1960), No. 4, 77-104.

KLEMPERER, VIKTOR. "Komik und Tragikomik bei Molière," *Die Neueren Sprachen,* XXX (1922), 327-350.

KNÖRRICH, OTTO. "Tragödie und Komödie heute," *Welt und Wort,* IX (1954), 335-336.

LAMONT, ROSETTE C. "The Metaphysical Farce: Beckett and Ionesco," *The French Review,* XXXII (1959), 319-328.

———. "Death and Tragi-Comedy: Three Plays of the New Theatre," *Massachusetts Review* (Winter-Spring, 1965), 381-402.

LANCASTER, HENRY CARRINGTON. *The French Tragi-Comedy: Its Origin and Development from 1551 to 1628,* Baltimore: J. H. Furst Company, 1907.

LEO, ULRICH. "Pirandello: Kunsttheorie und Maskensymbol," *Deutsche Vierteljahresschrift für Literaturwissenschaft und Geistesgeschichte,* XI (1933), 94-129.

LESSER, S. "Tragedy, Comedy, and the Esthetic Experience," *Literature and Psychology,* VI (1956), 131-139.

LEYBURN, ELLEN DOUGLAS. "Comedy and Tragedy Transposed," *The Yale Review,* LIII (1964), 553-562.

LOEWENBERG, J. *Dialogues from Delphi,* Berkeley: University of California Press, 1949.

MANDEL, OSCAR. *A Definition of Tragedy,* New York University Press, 1961.

NICOLL, ALLARDYCE. *The Theory of Drama,* New York: Crowell, n.d. (1931).

OLSON, ELDER. *Theory of Drama,* Detroit: Wayne State University Press, 1961.

ORTEGA Y GASSET, JOSÉ. "The Nature of the Novel," *Hudson Review,* X (1957), 11-42.

PLESSNER, HELMUT. *Lachen und Weinen. Eine Untersuchung nach den Grenzen des menschlichen Verhaltens.* Second Edition. Berne: Francke, 1950.

PRONKO, LEONARD CABELL. *Avant-Garde: The Experimental Theater in France,* Berkeley: University of California Press, 1962.

QUAYLE, CALVIN KING. *Humor in Tragedy*, unpubl. doctoral dissertation, University of Minnesota, 1958.

RISTINE, FRANK HUMPHREY. *English Tragicomedy: Its Origin and History*, New York: Columbia University Press, 1910.

SPIVACK, CHARLOTTE K. "Tragedy and Comedy: A Metaphysical Wedding," *Bucknell Review*, IX (1960), 212-223.

SPOERRI, THEOPHIL. "Das Problem des Tragischen," *Trivium*, V (1947), 153-179.

STOLNITZ, JEROME. "Notes on Comedy and Tragedy," *Philosophy and Phenomenological Research*, XVI (1955), 45-60.

STYAN, J. L. *Elements of Drama*, Cambridge University Press, 1960.

———. *The Dark Comedy: The Development of Modern Comic Tragedy*, Cambridge University Press, 1962.

THOMPSON, ALAN REYNOLDS. *The Dry Mock*, Berkeley: University of California Press, 1948.

THURBER, JAMES. "The Future, If Any, of Comedy," (London) *Times Literary Supplement*, August 11, 1961, 512-513.

———. "The Case for Comedy," *The Atlantic*, November, 1960, 97-99.

VOLKELT, JOHANNES. *Ästhetik des Tragischen*, 2nd ed., München: Beck, 1906.

———. *System der Ästhetik*, II, München: Beck, 1910.

WAITH, EUGENE M. *The Pattern of Tragicomedy in Beaumont and Fletcher*, New Haven: Yale University Press, 1952.

WELLWARTH, GEORGE E. *The Theatre of Protest and Paradox: Developments in the Avant-Garde Drama*, New York: University Press, 1964.

INDEX OF AUTHORS

INDEX OF PLAYS

About the Author

KARL S. GUTHKE is Professor of German Literature at the
University of Toronto (Scarborough College). He received
his M.A. in 1953 from the University of Texas and his
Ph.D. in 1956 from the University of Göttingen, Germany. He taught at the University of California at Berkeley
from 1956 to 1965, during which time he rose from the rank
of instructor to full professor. In this ten-year period, he
published a large number of articles in professional journals,
as well as several books on German and comparative literature. A collection of some of his essays will appear next year
as *Wege zur Literatur*.

SOME OTHER WORKS BY KARL S. GUTHKE

Englische Vorromantik und deutscher Sturm und Drang,
    1958.
Das Leid im Werke Gerhart Hauptmanns (co-author Hans
    M. Wolff), 1958.
Geschichte und Poetik der deutschen Tragikomödie, 1961.
Gerhart Hauptmann: Weltbild im Werk, 1961.
Haller und die Literatur, 1962.
Der Stand der Lessing-Forschung, 1965.